Make Up Your Mind

UNLOCK YOUR THOUGHTS,
TRANSFORM YOUR LIFE

DENISE PASS & MICHELLE NIETERT

Randall House • 114 Bush Road • Nashville, Tennessee 37217

Endorsements

"Yes, these 10 'mindsets' that Denise and Michelle write about are real. And yes, you (like me) may find yourself being a combination of two or more. But what I found incredibly helpful was learning how mindsets CAN change. From the mindset moments at the end of each chapter, to an unfolding understanding of how we really can have the mind of Christ in our everyday lives—let this team of life-change experts bring you the wisdom they've used to impact literally hundreds of lives. Unleashing you to find the freedom and rest for your mind and soul you've been longing for."

John Trent, Ph.D.
Author of *LifeMapping* and Co-Author of *The Blessing*
President, StrongFamilies.com

"Our mindsets matter! As a board-certified clinical neuropsychologist, I can tell you we all have somewhere between 50-70,000 thoughts daily and yet Scripture tells us to take every thought captive. That can seem overwhelming. Letting our thoughts run rampant and unchecked offers the enemy of our soul a playground for destruction and defeat. *Make Up Your Mind* offers the insight and strategies to unlock your defeating thoughts and positively transform your life for your good and God's glory. Denise Pass and Michelle Nietert have teamed up to help the reader identify the most common negative mindsets and exchange them for the healthy mindsets that reflect a sound mind. You'll want to reread this book time and time again."

Dr. Michelle Bengtson, author of the award-winning
Breaking Anxiety's Grip: How to Reclaim the Peace God Promises
and host of the award-winning podcast,
Your Hope Filled Perspective with Dr. Michelle Bengtson

"The alarm moments of life in today's culture are more the norm than the exception. Pass and Nietert's *Make Up Your Mind* provides a solid and timely biblical approach to the 'renewing of our minds.' Each chapter addresses some of the most common issues of our society. I highly recommend this biblically-based and practical work."

Neil Gilliland, Ph.D., director of member care, IM Inc.

"*Make Up Your Mind* offers keen biblical insights and practical tips regarding life's biggest battle—the battle of the mind. Pass and Nietert discuss ten negative mindsets that can drag us down and dismantle each one by highlighting the root issues and triggers that take us into a negative headspace. Using Scripture as their foundation, the authors help readers live victoriously through relatable sharing, practical tips, and "mindset movements" that aid believers in adopting the mind of Christ. A must-read!"

Michelle Pokorny, MACE, D.Min., adjunct professor for
Doctor of Ministry Studies, Dallas Theological Seminary

"We face challenges on all fronts—the lasting negative impact of the pandemic, nations in conflict, marriages in crisis, addictive behaviors, stressful jobs, debilitating grief, unexpected discouragement, and overwhelming hopelessness. If you or someone you know needs help, look no further. *Make Up Your Mind* will give you the tools you need to transform your thought-life, break free of energy-draining patterns, and apply biblical truth to your situation. This book provides practical help that will renew your faith and change your life for the better."

Carol Kent, executive director of Speak Up Ministries
Speaker and Author of *He Holds My Hand: Experiencing God's Presence and Protection*

"I'm an avid believer that controlling our thoughts and overcoming negative thinking is a game-changer when it comes to enjoying the life God has given us. In Make Up Your Mind, Denise identifies every negative mindset most people deal with at one time or another and gives practical strategies for learning to change your thoughts one step at a time. We can't always change our circumstances, but we can always change our patterns and habits of thinking, which in turn changes our lives for the better and Denise's powerful words and Michelle's wise counselor tips in the counselor's corner can help you do exactly that."

Tracie Miles, Best Selling Author
Author of *Unsinkable Faith: God-Filled Strategies for Transforming the Way You Think, Feel and Live*

"This book is loaded with techniques to combat negative mindsets that plague us. The reader will learn the triggers that get us off track and find helpful guidance on developing a godly mindset. I highly recommend it."

Edward E. Moody, Ph.D.,
author of *First Aid for Your Emotional Hurts*
Executive Secretary, National Association of Free Will Baptists

Dedication

I thank You, Jesus, and dedicate this work to You. Thank you for the profound worship and insights that abounded, which were life changing. I also dedicate this book to you, my beloved husband, who held up my arms, so to speak, so I could devote and dedicate myself to the work of this project, which included supporting my desire to pursue degrees at the same time.

Denise

I dedicate my Counselor's Corner to my mother, Ellen Holman. Mom, your love for God, His Word, and the power of prayer has been a constant inspiration to me and women around the world. Thank you for being such a faithful servant who has lived a life of desiring daily to experience the mind of Christ in all you do.

Michelle

Acknowledgements

No book such as this one could ever be written if there were not first encounters with God through life experience and inspiration that interrupted and affected us profoundly. We thank God for the gift of both His Word and His Holy Spirit. Without which, we would be lost, and our minds could not be renewed. Special thanks to our agent Blythe Daniel, the D6 Conference team, and Randall House. Thank you for your incredible support and partnership. Thank you to my friends who were willing to read the initial manuscript, I am grateful for your encouragement! And to my friend Michelle, thank you for partnering with me and going on this wild adventure with me! The late-night texting, phone calls, crying and laughing—it has indeed been worth it all! Truly this book is better with both of our voices urging on the readers as they defeat negative mindsets and learn to walk in the mind of Christ.

I (Michelle) am grateful to Denise and her passion for the mind of Christ. I thank the Community Counseling Associates staff for their support and my numerous author friends (including Mary DeMuth, Liz Rasley, and Leslie Wilson) who read, edited, and brainstormed this content with me. My sister Melissa Spoelstra offers me daily encouragement and accountability to the calling of writing. I can't imagine being on this journey without her. Special thanks to Reggie McNeal and Louie Giglio for allowing God to use you to teach me these truths in my early adult years. As I finished my last words, tears leaked from my eyes as I reflected on the faces of previous counseling and coaching clients whose sessions God brought to mind as I wrote. Though I cannot mention you by name, your willingness to bravely share and conquer these mindsets has made a lasting impression on me and now others.

Denise & Michelle

Table of Contents

Introduction

"Then he continued, 'Do not be afraid, Daniel. Since the first day that you set your mind to gain understanding and to humble yourself before your God, your words were heard, and I have come in response to them" (Daniel 10:12, NIV).

Throughout the pages of Scripture, we see the drama of the human condition played out as people succumbed to negative mindsets and tragedy ensued. We, too, can feel powerless when our own thoughts are deceptive, and we don't know how to change them. We can make excuses or blame others when our minds are overcome with negative mindsets. But the blame game does not heal our broken mindsets. And we don't have to be enslaved to our thoughts anymore. We can make up our mind to seek understanding through the mind of Christ.

Several years ago, God placed this book on my heart as I witnessed the destruction of people's lives because of what they wrongly believed. Having a healthy mindset is the key to a victorious life. I've seen a lot of defeated people who are operating in thoughts they seem unable to overcome. Why are some walking in victory and some not? Are we missing something?

Mindsets develop from thoughts and spiritual strongholds that we allow to supersede God's Word. When we believe our thoughts over God's, we travel to dangerous mental territory. The culture around us blindsides us with negative mindsets, worldviews, and social pressures. We don't think to question them because negative mindsets are the norm, and they influence and trap us. Thoughts seem to be true. They are inherent within our own mind. But God has placed His Holy Spirit within to help us resist the sin of negative mindsets.

The mind of Christ is formed within us by the same Holy Spirit who enabled Christ to walk in the Spirit and not the flesh. The disposition of Christ—His humility, joy, and countenance—are formed in us during the sanctification process as we yield to Christ's mindset and not our own.

My hope and prayer for us, dear readers, is that God will open our eyes to negative mindsets that have dominated us, and we will be set free and learn how to walk in the mind of Christ. Like Peter, we might feel like we're trying to walk on water at first, but the freedom that comes from walking in the Spirit instead of the flesh is what God intends for us. And the good news is that He will complete the work that He has begun in us.

As we read about each negative mindset, there is no condemnation if any of the mindsets currently "fit." Instead, we can put on gratefulness because we can now be set free. In each chapter, I share Scriptures and examples of people in the Bible who encountered the same mindsets. Most importantly, we see how Jesus handled each mindset and uncover how we can live into the mind of Christ. At the end of the first chapter there is a quiz you can take to help you determine your mindset struggle: **bit.ly/mindset-battle-quiz**. This is not to define you, but to help you to learn how to overcome it. We can make up our minds, friends, one thought at a time.

Denise

As a licensed professional counselor sitting across from women on my couch for over 20 years, I designed the "Counselor's Corner" to give a glimpse into the strategies that have created lasting life change in my office. I want to start by asking God to join with us, providing us with hope, and energizing us to believe that we can think, feel, and act differently.

Next, I want to provide practical tools and resources we can grab hold of to implement these changes. One of these tools is the Mindset Movement assignments at the end of each chapter. In my counseling office waiting room hangs a sign that says, "The other six days, 23 hours," to remind clients of the work mindset change requires.

I hope as you read this book you will know I am praying for you and cheering you on, confident of the work God will do in and through you.

Michelle

Chapter One

Why Are You Here?

"Answer me, LORD, answer me, so that this people may know that You, LORD, are God, and that You have turned their heart back."

—1 Kings 18:37, NASB

Driving to the airport, my stomach was in knots. Flying is not my favorite pastime, putting it mildly. No matter how many times I have tried to convince myself that flying is safer than driving, I always have to make up my mind to fly. I was on my way to an amazing opportunity—a television interview for my book, "Shame Off You"—in Canada, but my gnawing stomach betrayed the smile on my face.

Leaving my family and flying on a plane was scary and hard. I wished I could be as brave as others. While psychoanalyzing myself in bumper-to-bumper traffic, the battle in my mind was reaching a breaking point where I had to decide if I was going to give in to the fear or get on the plane. Right then, my phone rang, and after some pleasantries the voice said, "You have melanoma. We will need to do surgery. But the surgeon's first available appointment is over a month away. I'm sorry."

Times like these are defining moments in our lives. When what we dread happens, our mindset can determine how we process our pain. The week before I had gone in to check on a little bump on my head. And now this? In a moment, I was thinking about my dear husband ... my children ... how long I would have to live ... how much pain I would go through ... and the plane waiting for me.

With sweaty palms I changed traffic lanes, trying to figure out which lane would take me to the airport's economy parking. Then I accidentally crossed over into the oncoming lane and caught the attention of a police officer. I turned into the first parking lot, figuring the police officer would follow and pull me over. Instead, he passed me, and I could not find the stinkin' parking lot.

At this point, my mind was nearing freak-out mode. As I finally found the correct parking lot, boarded a shuttle, and advanced through the TSA pat-down, an announcement signaled a gate change. My flight had changed to a smaller airplane. WHAT?!

"Oh no, not a small plane again," said a nearby traveler. "The last one felt like a roller coaster."

Did I mention that I hate roller coasters? Packed on the bus awaiting transfer to the smaller plane, I contemplated how I could escape. I thought about the cancer diagnosis. Panic was beginning to overtake rational thinking as the battle in my mind began to escalate.

"Oh, God," I prayed. "Help me to trust you right now. I'm afraid. I can't do this. Please help me overcome my fears."

Hit Pause.

Life can change in a moment, and so can our mindsets. Circumstances and thoughts can be weighty. One moment we are all right, and the next moment we are filled with fear or anxiety because of a diagnosis or a loss or an unknown. How we handle our thoughts determines whether we will be in control of our mind or a victim of negative mindsets. When we are overwhelmed with negative thoughts, we do not have to continue down that path. We can pause and pray. We can choose what we think on, knowing that our thoughts matter.

The course of our lives is impacted by our thoughts. Our mind is where we decide to believe in or reject God. Under attack from the enemy of our soul or other influences, we must guard ourselves, so our thoughts don't throw us off course and send us to a place we never intended. Learning how to recognize thoughts that hold us captive, we can make those thoughts obedient to God's Word.

Just because we think something does not mean we have to believe it. We can overcome life's battles by overcoming our negative mindsets. "We demolish arguments and every pretension that sets itself up against the knowledge of God, and we take captive every thought to make it obedient to Christ" (2 Corinthians 10:5, NIV). It's a decision we must make.

Mind Over Matter

If mindsets were something we could easily choose, I'm pretty sure we would always pick the happy ones—you know, positive and cheerful. But mindsets are formed over time, in the shadowed recesses of scattered and often incoherent thoughts, provoked by life choices and difficult consequences. Without realizing it, in that place where emotions often clash resulting in mistaken and erroneous beliefs, negative mindsets can take over. However, rather than being a victim of our mindsets, we can drill down and keep asking questions until we discover why we are trapped in unproductive thought patterns.

For instance, certain scenarios in life evoke negative thoughts. If someone asks me to do something I hate to do, giving into that initial negative thought is a temptation. Somewhere there is a lie I am believing that keeps me trapped in a negative emotion. But if I keep asking questions, I can determine the root cause or stronghold I am really dealing with. If we form a habit of questioning our impulses, we don't have to be governed by them.

We must make up our mind to protect our belief system. The process of examining our thoughts is best done in concert with our Creator. As we ask Him to reveal the truth, He will do it. "Examine me, O Lord, and test me. Evaluate my inner thoughts and motives" (Psalm 26:2, NET). Foundational to overcoming negative mindsets is learning how to think for ourselves.

Think About It

The ability to think for ourselves affects our ability to overcome the battles of the mind. Sources differ on the number of thoughts or decisions we make in a day, some say up to a whopping 35,000 conscious decisions each day, give or take. We decide big things: our job, our spouse, our friends. And we pack our brains with small choices as well: what to eat, what to wear. We don't want to miss out on the satisfaction that comes from choosing well. However, there's the added pressure of pleasing others, the daunting influences of non-biblical worldviews, marketing, and social media surrounding us. Thinking for ourselves becomes quite complicated. But God has not left us alone in this battle.

Somewhere in our mental minefield is an inner voice guiding us. However, we can easily miss it if we're listening to the noise all around us instead. Our minds are our own, yet we can certainly struggle to make our minds up in accordance with the Word of God, which promises to renew them and lead us in truth. Solomon reminds us of the necessity of this truth, "Trust in the LORD with all your heart; do not depend on your own understanding. Seek his will in all you do, and he will show you which path to take" (Proverbs 3:5-6, NLT). Our own thoughts are faulty. We need revelation from God and a dependency on His righteousness, His thoughts, to be able to think rightly.

The Struggle Is Real

Negative mindsets gain the upper hand over our belief system because we don't often pause long enough to consider how they got there. Or we give up, weary of the struggle. This battle is further complicated by the spiritual warfare all around us. We can impulsively follow our emotions rather than choose a godly mindset.

Sometimes we are not convinced we can change our mind. It feels too hard. We have formed habits of thinking and don't know how to change. But we need to remember we *get* to choose. We can stay in the fight. The struggle is real, but God has not left us alone in the struggle. If we give up fighting, discouragement can lead us down a road to outright depression, and we might even find ourselves feeling like Elijah.

A Lesson from Elijah

Elijah had a mindset zealously set on God that caused him to boldly defend God in the face of fear. God's prophets were hiding out in caves due to the persecution of Jezebel, the wife of King Ahab. At God's command Elijah boldly went to meet King Ahab to challenge all the followers of Baal to decide between the one true God and Baal.

The odds were stacked against Elijah—one prophet of God against 450 prophets of Baal and their followers. Elijah did not waste time trying to change the opinions of the people around him. Elijah challenged the followers of Baal to make up their mind:

> "... "How long are you going to struggle with the two choices? If the Lord is God, follow Him; but if Baal, follow him." ... Then you call on the name of your god, and I will call on the name of the Lord; and the God who answers by fire, He is God." And all the people replied, "That is a good idea." (1 Kings 18:21, 24, NASB).

The boldness of Elijah to confront pagans was fueled by a faith in God that invited miracles. Elijah prayed a prayer so bold that it lit a fire of faith in the hearts of the people even as they watched fire come down from Heaven:

> "Answer me, O Lord, answer me, that this people may know that you, O Lord, are God, and that you have turned their hearts back." Then the fire of the Lord fell and consumed the burnt offering and the wood and the stones and the dust, and

> licked up the water that was in the trench. And when all the people saw it, they fell on their faces and said, "The LORD, he is God; the LORD, he is God." (1 Kings 18:37-39 ESV).

All the people changed their minds—not just some, all. What an incredible transformation. Placing our hope in Christ is sufficient to overcome even the strongest of mindsets.

But mindsets tend to drift, even with a man of God like Elijah. Even after mighty victories, Elijah's weak spot was breached by the enemy. Threatened by the evil wife of Ahab, terror gripped Elijah's heart as he fled for his life. What could make Elijah, so victorious one moment, run from a woman the next? A mindset change.

There in a cave hiding, Elijah turned to thoughts of fear and desperation, the opposite of his previous mindset of faith and power. What we focus on becomes our mindset.

> "He went and sat down under a shrub and asked the LORD to take his life: 'I've had enough! Now, O LORD, take my life. After all, I'm no better than my ancestors.' ... Suddenly the LORD's message came to him, 'Why are you here, Elijah?' He answered, 'I have been absolutely loyal to the LORD God of Heaven's Armies, even though the Israelites have abandoned the covenant they made with you ... I alone am left and now they want to take my life" 1 Kings 19:4b, 9b-10 (NET).

Elijah was done. Even so, God brought him sustenance so he could travel for 40 days and nights. This was another miracle, yet Elijah still had his excuses. In 1 Kings 19:13, God met Elijah again with His presence and the same question but in a whisper that invited him to rise above: "Why are you here, Elijah?"

Elijah gave the same answer. Even after encountering the living God through miracles, Elijah's mind was made up. This is what a mindset is: It is set on a particular thought, idea, or belief system that captivates us, not letting us go. When we allow lies or negative thoughts to dominate our mind, we lose perspective and lose our way.

Elijah, a man God used to change the minds of masses, made up his mind to allow fear and despair to have free rein. But God was not through with Elijah yet. He would use Elijah to mentor Elisha. God's directives for our lives and His grace to get us there are greater than the limits we have in our mind.

The Measure of a Man

We have all had times when we felt like we have just had enough. I have—like that day on the way to the airport when I was overwhelmed with my thoughts. We face moments in our lives when we can choose to overcome negative mindsets and discouragement or be engulfed by them. In those moments when we feel discouraged, we decide to give up or fight.

Often God asks us questions to make us aware of our mindset battle. Sometimes we don't want to fight because we just don't feel like we have the strength. But giving up means we gradually give way to a mindset that could define and entrap us for the rest of our lives. It is important to remember we don't have to fight mindsets in our own strength. God *is* with us. The turning point can be as simple as an utterance, a heart cry to God when we confess our dependence upon a broken mindset and ask God to help us overcome.

Jerry Falwell's statement has been one that has risen in my soul time and again when discouragement has threatened to cause me to lose perspective. "A man's greatness is measured not by his talent or his wealth, but by what it takes to discourage him."[1] If discouragement limited Elijah, it can limit us, too. But we can resist discouragement by learning how to adopt the mind of Christ when negative mindsets beset us. We will explore fully what that means.

What is discouraging us today? What are our minds focused on right now? We can breathe and reflect on our convictions and decisions. How did we get to the place we are now? We are not stuck. There is a way out. We can make up our mind differently and for the advancement of God's kingdom and glory. We just need to know how.

Winning the Battle of the Mind

When we stay in a mindset, we want to justify it. Even though we like to think our thoughts are right, we need to examine them and discover what triggers our negative mindsets. Then we will be able to develop tips and strategies for correcting course.

God wants to meet us with His Word at our place of mental struggles to heal and redeem them with freedom. "Do not be conformed to this world, but be transformed by the renewal of your mind, that by testing you may discern what is the will of God, what is good and acceptable and perfect" (Romans 12:2, ESV).

The word "mind" appears 762 times[2] in 13 translations of the Bible, and the word "thoughts" appears 195 times.[3] Our thoughts matter to God, and how we process our thoughts affects our lives and determines our ability to win the battles in our mind. Having our thoughts line up with the Word of God helps us to renew our mind. For those who have placed their faith in Jesus Christ, the Bible says we have the mind of Christ (1 Corinthians 2:16). Though we already have this available to us, many of us struggle to operate in the mind of Christ because we don't really know what that means.

Having the mind of Christ means operating from our identity as a child of God and deciding to adhere to mindsets Jesus demonstrated. Having Christ's mind also means we cast aside those mindsets Jesus didn't approve of and follow His example. We can have peace in the middle of chaotic thoughts. As we explore how Christ responded to the various negative mindsets we address in this book, we will learn how to respond similarly. It seems simple, but it's difficult to do. First, we can look at what keeps us from believing that Christ has the answers.

Trigger 1: Culture

We are all influenced in some way by peer pressure from our culture, luring us to follow its seductive ways, values, and beliefs. Every day our culture attempts to form our mindsets. The tactic of the enemy is that if he can get us to say or think something enough times, it becomes "truth." We need to hold on to God's truth while filtering out the messages, philosophies, and worldviews contrary to the Word of God that impact our mind and heart. If we don't make up our mind, others will do it for us.

Trigger 2: Self-Focused Mentality

We've all heard the following advice: Be you. There's only one you. Be true to yourself. That may sound good on the surface, and we definitely should be who God made us to be. But our own view of self can be skewed by negative mindsets and sin. These days we find ourselves engulfed in a self-focused society with misplaced self-expression. Paul knew this struggle all too well as he lamented the struggle against self (Romans 7:15).

When our mind is set on self, we cannot have a mindset that honors God. We cannot be the barometer for truth or have the final say when it comes to making up our mind. God's Word tells us to lean not on our own understanding (Proverbs 3:5-6). We need to give up being "true to ourselves" and be true to God and His Word.

Trigger 3: You've Got Personality

Our personality can make it challenging to make up our mind. But we can't blame mindset on our personality. I am a peacemaker by nature and love to serve others. This is part and parcel for being a momma, I think. But the peacemaker side of me impacts my ability to think for myself because peacemakers easily err toward becoming people pleasers. Understanding the weakness of what some would consider a strength helps me to guard my thoughts as I make decisions and overcome negative mindsets.

Each personality type has tendencies to gravitate toward certain mindsets. I used to consider myself shy and struggled with a mindset of timidity. I now recognize timidity, or a fear of people, robbed me of my calling. Our personality can influence our mindset, but our score on a personality test does not mean we are stuck. We get to choose.

Trigger 4: Mindsets

The English Oxford dictionary says a mindset is "an established set of attitudes held by someone."[4] This fixed state of mind makes for a closed mindset that is difficult to change. Some mindsets are positive and encourage growth, while other negative mindsets lead to entrapment and cause us to be dysfunctional. Mindsets matter because they impact our lives in dramatic ways, filtering our perception of life around us.

In following chapters, we will focus on negative mindsets we must battle as we seek to have the mind of Christ. Corresponding Scriptures will help us embrace alternative godly growth mindsets Christ wants us to have.

The Key to Making Up Our Mind

In a *Reader's Digest* article, "9 Split-Second Decisions That Changed History,"[5] by Beth Dreher and Claire Nowak, another side of a famous news story reveals the significance of how our decisions are impacted when we don't use the correct tools.

On April 14, 1912, a watchman on top of a large ship ran into a problem. To do his job he needed a pair of binoculars to see anything on the horizon that could pose a danger to the vessel. Only there was a dilemma: The binoculars were locked inside a trunk—and no one knew where the key was. It seems the ship's company made a last-minute crew change just before the ship left port, and someone forgot to hand off the key.

On that fateful day many mistakes led to the sinking of the Titanic and tragic loss of life: a shortage of lifeboats, not enough life jackets, bad weather, an iceberg—and a missing key. Over 1,500 people died as the unsinkable Titanic capsized. A simple key could have made the difference.

So it is with us. We hold the key to our mind. Do we use it? Do we lose it? If we were really convinced of how Scripture can help us overcome negative mindsets, we would apply the Word of God liberally. But so often we leave it locked away while we sink into negative thoughts. Our thoughts then turn into beliefs, and beliefs turn into action or inaction.

How We Make Decisions: Thinking for Ourselves

Changing negative mindsets requires us to be able to think for ourselves. The goal in thinking for ourselves is ultimately to think like Christ. Through studying the Bible, we develop the ability to think for ourselves with the following four essential tips that help us make up our mind regardless of circumstances.

Tip 1: Know Thyself

We know ourselves best when we know and understand the One who made us. Knowing ourselves in light of Scripture will enable us to make wise decisions not bound by mindsets. Mindset battles fade when we understand them through our identity as a child of God. We don't have to be afraid of knowing our weaknesses because we are not defined by them. We also can know our strengths and give God glory for them. As we recognize biases or preferences in ourselves as well as others, we can find biblical principles to support or oppose our point of view.

Tip 2: Work on Critical Thinking Skills

We are not all born with critical thinking skills. I know I wasn't. The good news is we can develop them. We must learn to think through our thoughts critically for our life is greatly impacted by them. "Be careful how you think; your life is shaped by your thoughts" (Proverbs 4:23, GNT).

Thinking critically means we are not gullible. Instead, we carefully and logically consider our way. "The simple believes everything, but the prudent gives thought to his steps" (Proverbs 14:15, ESV). God promises to give us wisdom when we ask (James 1:5), so understanding is always only a prayer away.

How do we think critically? By asking questions, by observing and evaluating thoughts against the plumb line of God's Word. We recognize flaws in our thinking by studying the One whose thoughts are perfect. Faced with real-life hard choices, emotions can make it difficult to discern the best answer. This is when an ability to think objectively can save us from a lot of pain. When we realize we can think with wisdom when aided by God's Word, it propels us and gives us confidence in our decision-making.

Tip 3: Examine Through a Biblical Worldview

Influence from the world, political correctness, and the fear of man can make thinking for ourselves difficult. Our thoughts need to be shaped from a biblical worldview based on eternity. Research from the Barna Group reveals only 4 percent of Americans (9 percent of born-again Christians) have a biblical worldview.[6] Individualism, humanism, and secularism, among many other philosophies and worldviews, have led us away from the truth and crippled our mindsets.

Our worldview becomes synonymous with our identity. When we know who we are in Christ, our mindsets form from that understanding. A biblical worldview is one in which Scripture is preeminent and infallible. God's Word has the final say on our thoughts. Confusion results when our mindset attaches to an everchanging worldview. Only through the perfect lens of Scripture can we see clearly.

Tip 4: Mindset Check

The words of the psalmist beautifully echo an examination of our thoughts we need daily. "Search me, O God, and know my heart! Try me and know my thoughts! And see if there be any grievous way in me, and lead me in the way everlasting!" (Psalm 139:23-24, ESV). We can learn to recognize when we are becoming entrapped by thoughts that perpetuate a victim mentality or that lead to bondage in sin if we are willing to examine our raw thoughts through the filter of God's Word.

Mindset of Christ

Scripture says we have the mind of Christ *now*. "For, 'Who can know the LORD's thoughts? Who knows enough to teach him?' But we understand these things, for we have the mind of Christ" (1 Corinthians 2:16, NLT). We have the mind of Christ, but we don't always operate like we do. In the upcoming pages we will see how putting on the mind of Christ helps us to make up our mind.

Mind Renewal: Keys to Unlock Our Mind

Key Thought:

We are not a victim of our mindset—we can choose our mindset. We are responsible for what goes in and settles there. Ultimately, when we place our thoughts under the lordship of Jesus Christ, our thoughts become like His.

Key Verse: Truth from God's Word

In Ephesians, Paul says we used to walk in our old ways of thinking, but we don't have to anymore once we are in Christ.

> And you He made alive, who were dead in trespasses and sins, in which you once walked according to the course of this world ... fulfilling the desires of the flesh and of the mind .... But now in Christ Jesus you who once were far off have been brought near by the blood of Christ (Ephesians 2:1-3, 13, NKJV).

Key Change: Application—Facing the Battle of the Mind

Take the "What's Your Mindset Struggle?" quiz.

We can't win the battle of the mind if we don't know the enemy we are facing. Now would be a good time to take the "What's Your Mindset Struggle?" quiz: **bit.ly/mindset-battle-quiz.** While we can all struggle with all the mindsets at any given time, this quiz will help you to recognize your chief negative mindset battle so you can then learn how to overcome it. Let's begin!

Counselor's Corner

We create our beliefs, and they evolve from our life experiences—from the messages we receive from others to the sights and sounds that surround us in our digital age. I often counsel women experiencing inner turmoil because they are losing the battle in their minds. Practicing a new consistent thought will create a fresh neurological pathway in our brains that gives that thought more priority. However, forming these new pathways takes dedicated time and practice.

When I sit with clients for the first time as they share their story, I listen for thoughts and life themes as they pour out past and current struggles. My first mindset intervention is so subtle they often don't realize they are shifting. As we talk, I slowly watch them begin to absorb hope that things can change. Combining hope with God's help enables us to overcome even the most traumatic life events. The first key is to believe in the possibility of transformation: not in a self-help "you can do this" mentality, but in a "God is bigger than your problem or situation, and His power works through you" mind shift.

One client shared, "I finally feel hopeful for the first time in two years." This client began to examine the false beliefs about herself that were making her miserable. Her sabotaging beliefs began to lose their power when she examined them out loud. The heavy load of the past lightens when we break the lies of shame and self-doubt and exchange them for positive truths based on who God says we are.

But how do clients create this freedom? Psychologists call it cognitive behavioral therapy. The Bible describes it as the "renewing of your mind" (Romans 12:2). When we implement scriptural principles to psychological interventions, we experience Holy Spirit empowered, life-changing results. This approach begins when we open our eyes each morning and embrace new thoughts. These new thoughts generate new feelings, which then often lead to new behaviors.

I often ask clients, "What do you want to feel when you wake up?" That leads to the next question, "What thoughts would you need to think to feel that way?" With God's help, we can become the conductor of our own thought train.

Neuroscience studies of brain patterns show that when we think new thoughts, we physically impact our brain. When we believe the good things God's Word tells us about ourselves, our world, and our God, we can begin to rewire our brains. Isn't that amazing?

What could happen in a year if we retrained our brains daily? Regularly rehearsing a biblical perspective of who we are empowers our faith-based "thought muscles" to become stronger. The result is our brain chemistry changes. We can then enter a maintenance stage, enjoying healthy thoughts and battling the temptations of negativity almost automatically when life events threaten.

Mindset Movement: *Choose one positive biblical thought to embrace about yourself or your life and practice it three times daily. I like using doorways as cues for reciting the new thought to myself as I build new, more positive neuropathways.*

Chapter Two

The Angry Mindset—Battling Bitterness and Unforgiveness

"For a man's anger does not bring about the righteousness of God."

—James 1:20, NASB

I always cry when I get angry, and it makes me so mad. My face breaks out in red bumps that look like hives, and I give in to the big old ugly cry. Frankly, it's embarrassing. That's not what anger is supposed to look like. Or is it? Perhaps crying out to God instead of letting that anger fall on people around me is a better way of handling anger.

The funny thing about anger is most people would not describe themselves as angry. I would say the same thing about myself, but like all the other negative mindsets in this book, all of us must deal with each of them on some personal level. And anger does not look the same on everybody.

Anger can encompass everything from rage and bitterness to unforgiveness and resentment or sometimes simply numbness if we can't deal effectively with conflicting emotions.

Anger can at times be displayed in a subtle fashion, but even so, its effects can be immense. If we do not deal with the mindset of anger biblically, James 1:20 says we cannot do the righteous things that God requires. This is a serious consequence for not dealing with anger.

The Look of Anger

I remember watching *The Incredible Hulk* as a kid. Something about how the Hulk's anger turned him into a massive beast fascinated me. He was powerful and strong, and no one could hurt him or those he was protecting.

I secretly always hoped someone could break through his angry persona though, because although being strong is admirable, out-of-control anger can hurt others. Lo and behold, those breakthroughs did happen on some episodes. Someone—usually an attractive female—was able to soothe his anger and help him to come back to earth, so to speak. I guess I wished I could have had the same effect on my dad when I disobeyed.

My earliest remembrance of anger was as a child. No one wanted to get Dad mad. I could see his flaring nostrils from across any room. The nauseous feeling in my stomach told me there was no way out once I knew I had been caught.

"Come here," he'd say in a tone that was terrifying enough. "Go get a belt."

As my heartbeat pounded in my chest, I tried to think of ways to avoid his wrath. Could his anger be soothed? Once I thought humor might be a good approach. Reaching for a silk belt from a robe, I smiled and brought it to my dad. He was not so amused. I still remember the spanking I got that day.

Now as a parent of five children, I understand why my dad was so angry. Discipline is just as hard on the adult as it is the child. I, too, have had my own moments of ire when my children have disobeyed or disrespected me, and I have thought about how I felt as a kid. Discipline is a necessary part of life, but how it is carried out can leave an imprint on a child's emotional development.

Discipline and anger do not have to go together. As my children grew up, I realized the anger I felt when I disciplined them had a root cause. Anger would arise in me when I took my children's behavior personally. This is one of the main hallmarks of anger. It is personal. It emerges when someone does something to us—hurts, minimizes, or simply bugs us.

It's Not About Me

As a parent I realized I needed to help my children with their behavior without viewing the incident as being about me. When I feel anger, it's usually because their behavior hurt my feelings or aggravated me repeatedly. I have learned I need to give myself time to process my feelings, which looks like sending the misbehaving culprit out of the room while I pray and ask God for wisdom to deal with their sin and mine. I don't have to yield control of my emotions to my children.

Realizing other people's sins or mistakes aren't always about me helps me to respond pragmatically and deal with the real sin problem at hand. When my children disobey me, they are being held hostage to their flesh and are rebelling against God. This matters a whole lot more than their breaking my rules.

Anger can turn into victimhood if we are not careful. We can feel justified in our anger and allow it to take over our minds.

However, anger cannot satisfy or heal our places of pain. Anger can easily fester into more than simply a momentary lapse of self-control; it can become a habitual mindset that defines us unless we learn how to process and master it. Understanding the root cause of our anger can help us stop it in its tracks.

Anger's Birth

Anger can present itself on a broad spectrum of outward manifestations. It can be silent, as bitterness or unforgiveness eat away at our joy. Or anger can be on the other end of the spectrum, where it is unleashed as full-fledged rage. Many of us might display our anger somewhere in between, but regardless of how we display our anger, at its root is an offense. Then when pride is fused with an offense, anger can become quite volatile and poisonous.

Feelings of anger do not have to dominate us. We can control moments of ire as we learn how to process them biblically and form new habits. Exposing resentment and unforgiveness can change our perspective and remind us what matters most. But what is anger exactly? What makes us fly off the handle with passion? Can anger truly be tamed?

Are We Mad?

Giving in to an angry mindset can cause us to lose perspective on reality. The Oxford Dictionary helps us out with some definitions for the word "mad" that might give us pause the next time we want to give full vent to our anger.

- "In a frenzied mental or physical state."
- "Extremely foolish; not sensible."
- "Completely insane; crazy."[7]

None of those definitions for mad would make us want to identify as having an anger problem, right? Scripture does not speak highly of anger either: "The wise fear the Lord and shun evil, but a fool is hotheaded and yet feels secure. A quick-tempered person does foolish things, and the one who devises evil schemes is hated" (Proverbs 14:16-17, NIV).

While we all have moments of anger, patterns of anger can become habitually dysfunctional. However, when we learn to counter anger with a healthy response rather than giving into this mindset, we can tame anger rather than letting it rule us. Understanding the root of our anger helps us dig it out of our lives effectively. Where does our anger come from? Whether it emanates from injustice, hurt, or covetousness, anger does not have to define us.

Anger Arising from Injustice

Anger is an uprising within us that cries out, "Not fair!" Springing from a sense of entitlement, anger causes us to demand what we feel we deserve. Most toddlers readily demonstrate this type of anger. In their world, there is comfort in things going as planned, and they let us know when things don't go accordingly.

Adults feel this pain, too—when events do not go as predicted, when we don't get what we expected. But life isn't fair. This fallen world is not Heaven. Yet somehow in this messy, uncertain life, we must navigate through many unfair outcomes.

This does not mean we take everything sitting down. There is a righteous anger for injustice that Scripture allows us to have. "Speak up for those who cannot speak for themselves; ensure justice for those being crushed" (Proverbs 31:8, NLT). Nevertheless, this righteous anger is still no excuse to let anger fly. Being led of the Spirit and responding like Christ, we can help be a light to this world and leave vengeance in God's hands.

Anger Arising from Hurt

Broken trust, cruelty, infidelity, or betrayal wound us deeply, sometimes rendering us unable even to exhibit the anger underneath. Such hurts can leave us not knowing how to respond. Years ago, I found myself sitting on the proverbial couch with a shriveled tissue in my hand. My counselor was prodding me to express the anger I felt. I sobbed profusely. The revelation of my ex-husband's sexual abuse of some of our children had put me in a state of shock and fear. I struggled greatly with how to express my anger.

Being hurt by others produces a twist in the anger we feel. We feel powerless and boxed in by our intense emotions. It is natural to feel anger when we have been hurt. It would be unnatural not to. But there is a way to process anger that helps us remain in control, rightly recognizing the roots of the anger we are feeling. Yielding our passionate feelings of anger to God and asking for His help releases us from anger's grip.

In my example, instead of dwelling on the pain, I chose to dwell on God's promises. Instead of choosing unforgiveness and resentment, I poured out my pain to the God who sees and trusted Him to defend and heal my pain. It is hard work, friends. So hard. But being in bondage to anger is harder still.

Seeking to understand the root of our anger sets us free from its wrath. "Whoever is slow to anger has great understanding, but he who has a hasty temper exalts folly" (Proverbs 14:29, ESV). Slowly I let go of the anger directed at a person and began the work of forgiveness. The sins committed still impact my life and the lives of my children. This reality hurts more than I can adequately express. But anger won't heal our hurts. Giving our anger to God and letting Him renew and heal our mind will. We don't have to stay in the mindset of anger, even when it feels justified.

Anger Arising from Covetousness

Jealousy and covetousness are common sources of anger. Where two or more are gathered, there is comparison. Cain demonstrated what can happen when covetousness and jealousy grip a heart and are not dealt with in a healthy manner. Murdering his own brother was obviously a vile deed with severe consequences, but even on a smaller scale, anger arising from jealousy wrecks relationships and impacts our walk with God.

Anger from covetousness is like saying God's provision is not enough, that we want more than God's allotment for us. But God's Word reminds us that His boundaries for us lie in pleasant places. It is when we look outside those boundaries that the grass seems greener. That's when we forget what God has given us is for a specific purpose in our lives and is for His glory, not ours.

Chronic Anger

Situational anger can catch us off guard. If we aren't mentally ready for something, we may not know how to respond.

But being angry in a moment or a circumstance is different than being characterized as an angry person. Chronic anger can be learned behavior from an environment we grew up in. It can also be cultivated when we give into bitterness and unforgiveness because we simply do not know how to process life and relationships.

Anger becomes deep-seated when we stop trying to control anger and give in to its demands. Chronic anger can be aggressive or passive aggressive. We may use anger to control others or outcomes, and this becomes a dysfunctional way of relating to others.

We have all likely encountered the grumpy personality that grumbles or barks out his or her sentiments. People can cower or be intimidated by chronically angry people. We can say it is just their personality, but that is not the truth. All of us are accountable for the anger we permit in our lives.

We cannot be holy if we are bound in anger. This should motivate us to deal with anger in our lives so we don't become enslaved to it. We don't have to live with anger. We don't have to let it perpetuate or continue day after day. We can ask God to reveal what is behind the anger and deal with the heart of the matter. "Be angry and do not sin; do not let the sun go down on your anger" (Ephesians 4:26, ESV).

An Appropriate Anger Deserves an Appropriate Response

We might wonder if there is ever a proper place for anger. God gets angry. He constantly has to address the waywardness and sinfulness of His people. Yet God's anger is appropriate and deserved. In contrast, our anger is often self-righteous rather than righteous. However, at times we may experience appropriate anger, as well. When my children sin, an appropriate response is to deal with the sin. An inappropriate response is to go ballistic for the behavior and resent them for it. At such times it is helpful for me to live by this verse: "A soft answer turns away wrath, but a harsh word stirs up anger" (Proverbs 15:1, ESV).

A Lesson from Moses

If the humblest guy in the world could not quell anger during one intense dilemma, then perhaps we, too, have had moments when we unleashed anger rather than taming it. Moses' striking of a rock in anger in the presence of God and His people was enough to cost him the prize of entering the Promised Land. This was a big consequence for a momentary fault of fury. Why did Moses' angry slip cost him so much?

God's people were quarreling and grumbling against Moses and Aaron because they had been led into the desert where there was no water. This angry mob caused this wandering in the desert in the first place—all because of their lack of faith in the God who had saved them. "And the Lord said to Moses, 'How long will this people despise me? And how long will they not believe in me, in spite of all the signs that I have done among them?'" (Numbers 14:11, ESV).

God planned to destroy the people and make a nation from Moses. But Moses pleaded with God for mercy on behalf of the people based on God's character rather than theirs. God heard Moses, but there were consequences for the people's grumblings, lack of faith, and disobedience. "None of the men who have seen my glory and my signs that I did in Egypt and in the wilderness, and yet have put me to the test these ten times and have not obeyed my voice, shall see the land that I swore to give to their fathers. And none of those who despised me shall see it" (Numbers 14:22-23, ESV).

Moses was a faithful shepherd of God's people. He had dealt with a lot of whining and complaining. But it was ultimately Moses' annoyance with the people's rebellion and his own lack of faith in God that unleashed his anger.

> "'... Hear now, you rebels: shall we bring water for you out of this rock?' And Moses lifted up his hand and struck the rock with his staff twice, and water came out abundantly, and the congregation drank, and their livestock. And the LORD said to Moses and Aaron, 'Because you did not believe in me, to uphold me as holy in the eyes of the people of Israel, therefore you shall not bring this assembly into the land that I have given them'" (Numbers 20:10b-12, ESV).

It was the people Moses dealt with day in and day out who provoked Moses to his out-of-control rage. And so it is with us. The people in our sphere whom we deal with every day are the ones we usually struggle with the most. We can take their groanings and grumblings personally—like with our children—and be angry because of the inconvenience of dealing with their behavior.

For the most part Moses demonstrated belief in God, but mindsets affect our belief system. Moses became focused on the people's grumbling and wasn't thinking about the preeminence of God's plans. We feel for Moses. It is hard to keep a correct perspective. But it is not impossible. When we are tempted to throw in the towel and let anger flare, we need to remember we are representing God. He is holy. Our belief in God's faithfulness to resolve what is making us angry speaks volumes to those around us. He is in control, not us. That is a humbling position. Like Moses, we can learn humility and can quell anger when we remember our position and stay on mission.

The Fruit of Anger

While caving to anger and bitterness might satisfy our deprived sense of justice, we reap a reward we don't want. Frederick Buechner, a twentieth-century American writer and theologian, vividly describes the fruit of anger in our lives:

"Of the 7 deadly sins, anger is possibly the most fun. To lick your wounds, to smack your lips over grievances long past, to roll over your tongue the prospect of bitter confrontations still to come, to savor to the last toothsome morsel both the pain you are given and the pain you are giving back—in many ways it is a feast fit for a king. The chief drawback is that what you are wolfing down is yourself. The skeleton at the feast is you."[8]

Anger hurts us, as well as others. Anger must be dealt with before the course of our lives is ruined. Examining the triggers leading to anger can help us think ahead before we give ourselves over to anger's dominion.

Trigger 1: Expectations

Moses did not expect the trip from Egypt to the Promised Land to take 40 years. It should have taken 11 days. Anyone could get angry about that realization. Circumstances can trigger anger as we try to control the uncontrollable and wonder why God isn't doing something about it. This was the same issue the people of God had. Would they trust God to get them to the Promised Land?

Have you ever been angry with God because of expectations? This is the crux behind our culture's distrust of God. The world's philosophy basically says if God were good, He would not allow suffering. Yet when we look at examples in Scripture as to what God ultimately brings about, we understand we don't have to be angry about things not going our way. It's better to have things go God's way than ours. His purposes are far greater, and His plans are always for our good and His glory.

The Old Testament's story about Naomi is another good example of a person's mindset turning to bitterness from failed expectations. However, the suffering God allowed for Naomi eventually led her daughter-in-law Ruth to be a part of the lineage of Jesus. God always redeems our messes. Getting angry does not heal us or fix our situation, but when we trust God with our messes, He uses them to bless us.

Trigger 2: Offense

The Israelites were angry with Moses and Aaron. I'm pretty sure Moses was also offended at the people's rebellion and attacks on Aaron and him. When we become offended, we become distracted with self, wishing we did not have to deal with our present situation. It is then we need to remember that God could have remained offended at us. We have no right to remain in anger against others when God has not remained angry with us. "Good sense makes one slow to anger, and it is his glory to overlook an offense" (Proverbs 19:11, ESV).

Trigger 3: Comparison/Coveting

Sometimes we don't even realize the source of our anger is comparison. For example, we all know people who do not have the same struggles as we may have. It seems everything comes so easily for them. Similarly, the Israelites were angry while wandering in the wilderness because they compared their current state to the comforts of their former Egyptian home. They grumbled that back in Egypt they had plenty of fish and root vegetables to eat. But the Israelites forgot an important part: Their former life was one of slavery. And they were complaining about not having enough onions.

Comparison can be so shortsighted; it doesn't consider the whole picture. Looking to the past or the present will not help us overcome anger. However, looking to the future that God has for us can. This world is not supposed to be our joy. God is.

Trigger 4: Shame

Shame is like a hot potato. People do not want to admit they have shame, so they hurl it onto someone else. Shame can evoke a prideful, angry response. Shame from childhood can cloud our existence because we never recognized it as shame and didn't know how to deal with it. The bullies of the playground or people who minimized us can cause us anger over such mistreatment, impacting our spirits for a lifetime. We will infect others with the shame we received if we do not process the anger caused by past abuse. Christ bore all our sin—and shame. He chose to come and suffer at the hands of the people He created to redeem them. When we suffer, too, at the hands of sinful people, we can look to Christ. Shame is a trap, stealing our worth. But Christ restored our honor, and shame does not get the final say.

Trigger 5: Control

Like the TV show *The Incredible Hulk,* sometimes anger can stem from control issues. We want things to be a certain way, and they are not. Different than having certain expectations, control issues happen when we cannot let go of our plan and then become spiteful over it. Understanding that God is in complete control helps us to relinquish the control we think we have. We never were in control in the first place. Adopting a servant's heart in our leadership helps us to let God lead through us instead. And letting go of trying to control outcomes releases the control that the mindset of anger has on us.

Anger's Consequences

Giving in to our anger has far-reaching consequences. For Moses, his rash anger with the Israelites meant that he would not enter the Promised Land, the very goal of his mission from God. For Cain, coveting his brother's position led to him murdering his brother and caused him to be a wanderer the rest of his life. For Saul, his jealous rage against David caused him to pursue David relentlessly and eventually lose his crown and life. Even Saul's sons suffered for their father's untamable anger. For Jonah, his anger at God almost caused him to miss God's mission for his life. In many of our experiences of anger, sin is there, provoking and igniting our emotions. However, God can help us overcome the passion of anger and channel it toward a passion for His glory instead.

Tip 1: Wisdom

Solomon was angry at the human condition, and he did not sugarcoat his struggles. He admitted his anger, confessed his thoughts, then decided to choose a different mindset once God revealed the flaw in his thinking:

"I devoted myself to search for understanding and to explore by wisdom everything being done under heaven. I soon discovered that God has dealt a tragic existence to the human race" (Ecclesiastes 1:13, NLT). "So I came to hate life because everything done here under the sun is so troubling. Everything is meaningless—like chasing the wind" (Ecclesiastes 2:17, NLT). "So I gave up in despair, questioning the value of all my hard work in this world" (Ecclesiastes 2:20, NLT). "So I decided there is nothing better than to enjoy food and drink and to find satisfaction in work. Then I realized that these pleasures are from the hand of God" (Ecclesiastes 2:24, NLT).

Notice the mindset shift. The saving grace for Solomon was his devotion to finding truth and a right understanding. He sought God. Solomon's initial observation was changed with a revelation from God. He went from despair and hate to understanding the blessings of God in his life, recognizing that God, not any earthly pursuit, was his central delight.

Sometimes we can get so fixated on what bugs us that we miss the blessings all around us. Work is a bummer to one, while another person wishes she had a job. One person complains about her children's behavior while another wishes she was able to have children. Our goal is not having a perfect life but knowing and thinking like the perfect One in this life. Solomon's key to wisdom was not accepting anger as his mindset. He sought to understand the root of his emotion. Anger did not have to control him. Wisdom set him free. "Fools vent their anger, but the wise quietly hold it back" (Proverbs 29:11, NLT).

Tip 2: Gratitude

Anger says we deserve better. But the truth is, we don't. Anger becomes embedded in our mind when we become fixated on the "coulda, woulda, shouldas" instead of looking around and noticing the good things we already have. I was in the hospital struggling with complications from COVID-19 when I learned a valuable lesson in gratitude. My mindset shifted away from one of anger as I reflected on all the blessings in my life.

I could have been angry at the person who got me sick. I could have been angry that I happened to be one of those people who had a bad reaction to the virus due to autoimmune problems. Or I could have been angry at the care I received. Instead, I was grateful. God enabled me to see the good He was accomplishing through the illness, and He reminded me I was on a kingdom mission right there in the hospital. It wasn't about me—about my inconvenience or suffering. It was about God and seeing His accomplishments through it all.

Putting on a different mindset made the anger disappear, leaving profuse gratitude and a hope rekindled by seeing the goodness of God in the land of the living (Psalm 27:13-14). Only God could do that, and gratitude was the catalyst that helped change my mindset.

Tip 3: Self-Control

Flipping out and getting angry might have been OK for the Incredible Hulk. He could get away with it because his anger always seemed justified—and, well, he was fictional. But we don't have to give in even to justified anger. We have a choice.

David was justified in his anger over Saul's constant pursuit and maligning of him. (Of course, David also had his own skeletons in his closet.) But David did not take revenge. As an old man, David had learned much from the drama he experienced during his life. He understood he did not have to contribute to the drama but could overcome it. David wrote the words of Psalm 37: "Refrain from anger and turn from wrath; do not fret—it leads only to evil" (Psalm 37:8, NIV).

Paul also challenged us to get rid of all anger, and we can take note of how he did it. "Be kind and compassionate to one another, forgiving each other, just as in Christ God forgave you" (Ephesians 4:32, NIV). That's right. We can be kind and compassionate, especially when we remember Christ's compassion toward us. Forgiveness enables us to let go of what is holding on to us.

Tip 4: Forgiveness

Unforgiveness keeps us bound in anger as we nurse grudges against others. Oftentimes, those who have hurt us might not even be aware we are angry with them. The ones who continue to carry anger are the ones who suffer the most.

So how can we forgive the unforgiveable? Are we just supposed to forget about heinous deeds done against us? No, but putting on Christ's perspective and hunting through Scripture for understanding helps us see that forgiveness does not give a pass for evil. However, ultimately, there is no forgiveness for us if we cannot forgive others. "But if you do not forgive others their sins, your Father will not forgive your sins" (Matthew 6:15, NIV).

Christ forgave us. We don't have a right to hold on to unforgiveness. Forgiving like Christ requires us to care about the offender, and it enables us to let go of the effects of evil done to us. As author Lysa TerKeurst wrote in *Forgiving What You Can't Forget*, "My ability to heal cannot be conditional on them wanting my forgiveness but only on my willingness to give it."[9]

Tip 5: Humility

Pride is the fuel behind anger. When we think we are above a situation or when we think we deserve better treatment, anger always seems to be lurking close by. However, humility has a way of putting out anger's fire. How can a prideful people be humble? Christ showed us the way, and He did it with joy. "… Fixing our eyes on Jesus, the pioneer and perfecter of faith. For the joy set before him he endured the cross, scorning its shame, and sat down at the right hand of the throne of God" (Hebrews 12:2, NIV).

Instead of looking at what provokes anger, we can look to Christ's example. He chose a humble path to get to our souls. He chose suffering that we seek to avoid. Humility gives us a perspective on anger that helps us realize how selfish it is in the first place.

Getting to the Root

We don't have to be characterized by an angry mindset. A mindset of anger is like an addiction fixated on the cause of our ire. When we fear not being able to make our outcome what we had envisioned, our anger tries to control the situation with tools of intimidation and complaints. But we can master our anger rather than being mastered by it when we examine it.

We can come to understand the triggers that cause it and choose a different, biblical response. We don't have to shoot arrows aimlessly at others around us. Examining our anger might mean we give ourselves a time out with God's Word and ask questions to find out why we are giving into the temptation to be bitter or angry.

The fruit of anger is ugly and it can also be deadly when not dealt with, affecting one's physical and mental health. Anger is passion run awry. It feels like it cannot be tamed, but it can. As we look to our Savior who felt anger Himself, we learn how to be angry and sin not. We wrestle with the tension of a righteous anger and a foolish one. Christ shows us how.

Mindset of Christ

When confronted with angry people, Jesus withdrew from the situation and did not defend Himself (Matthew 12:15; 16:4; John 10:39; Isaiah 53:7; Mark 15:5). Jesus did not fear them, and He did not back down from His message. He did not respond with pride, but humbly tried to reveal their need.

Friends, God turned away His anger toward us and placed it on His own Son. Think about that. We deserved His anger. It was a righteous anger, and we were His enemies. But "Through the LORD's mercies we are not consumed, because His compassions fail not" (Lamentations 3:22, NKJV). And the mercy of God's Son goes on and on. Christ forgave those who spat on Him, who scourged Him, who crucified Him—because He loved them. Christ's mind was steadfast on His love toward those who deserved His anger.

Can we do the same? Can we love those who offend us, hurt us, make us angry? It will require dying to self and having a kingdom mindset fixed on forgiveness and grace.

Mind Renewal: Keys to Unlock Our Mind

Key Thought:

We can choose to handle anger biblically when we recognize the root cause of our anger.

Key Verse: Truth from God's Word

"Get rid of all bitterness, rage and anger, brawling and slander, along with every form of malice. Be kind and compassionate to one another, forgiving each other, just as in Christ God forgave you" (Ephesians 4:31-32, NIV).

Key Change: Application— Releasing Anger and Finding Joy

There is good news in Paul's admonition for us to get rid of *all* bitterness, rage, and anger. He wouldn't have said it if we couldn't do it. Ask God to reveal anger in your life and to help you let it go. Journal about it as you examine the cause and effect and remember that just as God did not take out His wrath on us, He can also give us grace to release anger in Jesus' name.

Counselor's Corner

What's your anger style? Do you stuff your anger? Let it drip? Or when your fuse snaps, do you explode? Where do you feel it in your body, and how do you release it? These assessment questions help me as a counselor when working with counseling clients on anger management treatment plans. Feeling anger is a given, but we are called to be "slow to anger" (James 1:19) so we can better manage it.

This skill takes commitment and practice. It also requires the belief that *our* anger is always *our* problem. If we tend to say things like, "I know I ________, but you ________," it's time to erase the "but you." As we quit placing blame on others, we will be able to experience the freedom that comes from owning our own emotions, no longer giving our emotional control to other people.

I want to add two mindsets to your coping skill toolbox: flexibility and compassion. Flexible thinking allows us to bend with circumstances beyond our control, like a pipe cleaner. Bending like a pipe cleaner is better than snapping like a rigid craft stick any day! One way to increase our flexible thinking is to erase as many "shoulds" from our vocabulary and turn them into "coulds." This allows us and those around us to function as the flawed humans we are.

The next time you think, "He *should* understand me," change that thought to, "I wish he *could* understand me." Changing our "shoulds" to "coulds" shrinks the gap between expectations and reality, and in turn, diminishes the intensity of our emotional responses. Maybe a chronically late friend *should* be on time. But when she isn't, the quicker we accept the reality she is late, the more we can enjoy her company.

Scripture tells us that Jesus empathizes with our weaknesses (Hebrews 4:15). Counseling treatment plans that address anger almost always involve having compassion for others, including ourselves. Learning to practice compassion for others means acknowledging our own weaknesses, recognizing all of us do what we do not want to do (Romans 7:19), and realizing we can't always fix it. When forgiveness seems like a huge leap of faith, compassion for self and others can be a baby step that propels us in the right direction.

Dr. Kristin Neff, a researcher on self-compassion, has developed a quiz, tools, and exercises for counselors and their clients to begin embracing and practicing self-compassion. What would it be like if the next time we forget a deadline, find our home looking like a disaster, or even lose it with one of our kids, that before beating ourselves up, we intentionally directed our thoughts toward a stance of self-compassion?

It might sound like, "I'm doing the best I can, and that's good enough."

"Everyone makes mistakes, and I'm allowed to also."

"God still loves me, and it's all going to be OK."

Practicing self-compassion statements decreases the amount of internal anger we experience freeing us from the self-hatred that often leads to depression. Also, when we have less anger at ourselves stored in our bodies, less anger is likely to find its way into the lives of the people we love.

Mindset Movement: *Practice compassion the next time you or someone you love makes a mistake. Observe how it changes your internal feelings and physical body response.*

Chapter Three

The Anxious Mindset—Battling Fear and Worry, Restoring Peace

"In the multitude of my anxieties within me, your comforts delight my soul."

—Psalm 94:19, NKJV

The day my husband told me I was an anxious person I could not believe it. (Serious case of denial, y'all!) Oftentimes, we don't recognize the mindsets that plague us. This is what makes mindsets so powerful in the first place. Mindsets come and go, and sometimes we can blame a mindset on something that happened to us rather than realizing it has become a part of our character. Even though I am not someone who worries about everything, anxiety comes in many colors, and it has obscured the peace of God in my life. I ought to have known anxiety was something I struggled with. I had been told this once before.

Sitting in the doctor's office smiling and joking, I was trying to convince the doctor and myself that anxiety is for other people. But my cavalier demeanor did not work.

"You've got anxiety," the doctor said.

Then, as if those words finally gave me the freedom to admit it, the tears flowed from my eyes. Instinctively I knew it was true. But doggone it, I did not want to concede to that truth. Did anxiety make me less of a Christian? No. Christ experienced anxiety in the Garden of Gethsemane. He knew what it was like to be under great stress, but He also knew how to deal with anxiety.

Whether our mindset of anxiety arises from certain situations, social environments, traumatic events, or a disorder, there is hope. We don't have to stay there. We all have our own unique way of dealing with anxiety. Some might chew their nails (ew!). Others might twist their hair. Or when anxiety really has us in its grip, we can exhibit signs like breathlessness, heart palpitations, excessive worrying, mind racing, or sleeplessness, to name a few. Still, others might deny its existence and not recognize the effects and toll that anxiety is taking on them. However, burying our head in the sand will not reduce stress in our lives. Understanding what causes the anxious mindset can help us defeat it.

Situational Anxiety

The anxiety I am personally most familiar with is situational anxiety—anxiety that stems from things that happen to us in everyday life. One such situation that comes to mind is a time I found myself sitting in the basement with my children while wind from a nearby tornado roared outside. The window in the kitchen had bowed in, and we knew the system was close.

With a sense of excitement mingled with fear, my kids and I wondered what would happen. The howling wind stirred our anxiety, and the flickering lights had us all on alert. We did not want to give in to fear, but we did not want to be foolish either. Sometimes anxiety can save our lives. Anxiety can be a warning sign to us that something is not right. But when we cannot control anxiety and channel it to productive solutions, anxiety has us in its grip.

Then there are situations like a few years back when I traveled to Guatemala with Compassion International. This trip meant facing my fear of flying. Again. (See chapter one to see how this is still something I struggle with.) Symptomatic with the fear of traveling to a foreign country, my sweaty palms and rapid heartbeat were indicators that anxiety was trying to overtake my mind. Suddenly the plane dropped 1,000 feet (an 8 on a scale of 1-10, according to the pilot). People were screaming, and I was clinging to the seat for dear life. But instead of screaming or giving into fear, I prayed. I breathed long, deep breaths. I coached myself to compare the plane's bumps in the air to my car's bumps on the road. Then I put labels on the fear I was feeling: fear of falling, fear of heights, fear of being out of control, fear of suffering, fear of leaving loved ones, fear of dying.

Sometimes people shame others for their fears, saying they do not have enough faith. But if we are honest, we all wrestle with fear in one form or another. Unchecked, anxiety could keep me from going anywhere and from leading the life God directs me to live. That would not be a healthy response. However, although it is uncomfortable, I can choose to do hard things, and those hard choices help my fear to shrink.

Underlying both experiences of situational anxiety described above is the desire to be safe. I have been a "safe girl" my whole life, from stepping over cracks to avoiding roller coasters or anything else that looked potentially risky. Even though at first it might seem wise to be safe—I mean, careful sounds a lot better than careless—there is something behind this anxiety that reveals a lack of trust and a strong desire to avoid pain. Somehow, I was programmed to avoid any remote chance of discomfort to the point that it limited my life. Giving in to fear keeps us bound, imprisoning us in our circumstances. Facing fear sets us free.

The difficulty with combatting situational anxiety is that it is a strong, automatic emotional response that sends our adrenaline into overdrive. Our mind runs with thoughts of fear and desperation, and it feels like we cannot control these thoughts. But we can choose what we focus on and thereby experience captivity or freedom, fear or faith.

Though the emotion of anxiety is so very strong and automatic, we can still choose to take those thoughts and bring them to Jesus. We can recognize our anxious thoughts are often unrealistic, but more than that, we can run them through the Word of God. Finding Scripture to counter the worries of this life enables us to be in control of the impact anxiety has on us instead of it controlling us.

Social Anxiety

Social anxiety is plaguing today's generations due to the prevalence of living our lives in front of the world with social media. Since the beginning of time man has lived in fear of man's judgment, but this is heightened in a world where opinions of others can be aired and magnified many times over. Negative feelings of shame—not being enough or being insecure—limit our existence when we give sway to what other's opinions are of us over God's. In particular, the hearts of our youth have become gripped with anxiety stemming from their notion of how others perceive them.

This is something we can all struggle with. As a mom, it breaks my heart when I see my children distraught because someone said something negative to them or they feel someone treated them in an unkind manner. The fear of man is a trap, and it has snared many in our culture.

With the advent of social media, striving to seek the acceptance and approval of others has reached epic proportions. Social media is impacting the mental well-being of young adults today. Anxiety, depression, and low self-esteem are taking a toll on emerging young adults who can't seem to find their identity outside of their phones and social media, according to research about the relationship between social media use and social anxiety among this age group. Social media impacts and shapes a young person's identity.

Whether or not social media is the initial trigger of a person's social anxiety, there is a direct causal link between excessive use of social media and social anxiety. This can be remedied, but it is a hard fight. Social media is addictive. My oldest son recognized the toll social media was taking on him and chose to remove it from his phone. He now has very specific boundaries with social media because he felt it chip away at his confidence; it produced social anxiety in him.

Historically, social anxiety has always been a struggle for some because humans have always compared themselves to one another. However, social media has amped up the effect. In the end, what others think about us is a dangerous place to put our confidence. People's opinions are fickle and can never supplant God's truth about who we are.

Anxiety From Trauma

A traumatic event can leave such a damaging effect on our lives. Overwhelmed by the turmoil, it is easy to think we can never recover from it. I have experienced anxiety during several traumatic seasons of my life. Anxiety developed when I was a child as my parents managed multiple divorces and moves. All those changes affected my personality greatly as I struggled to approach life with confidence.

Later, anxiety developed after the revelation of betrayal and sin in my ex-husband's life. I wondered how I could move forward. But God. Then there has been anxiety from extreme health situations. In each of these traumatic events, when I was under great duress, anxiety threatened to snuff out any possibility of recovery. However, each time anxiety has been overcome by the grace of God.

The tips I share below are a significant part of how I applied the grace of God in my life. But guess what? Anxiety rises again and again in this crazy life. But now I know how to deal with it appropriately. All of us can with the biblical principles laid out in this chapter and the grace of God. We must not grow weary in well doing, friends. In due time, we will reap a harvest.

Anxiety Disorders

Some people are just wired to be more anxious. Call it genetic or environmental, such disposition toward anxiety is hard to let go of. Different personality types and temperaments have different weaknesses. But God is bringing us from glory to glory. We don't have to tolerate anxiety's presence.

This unacceptance might require a hard fight and a rewiring of our brain, but we don't have to continue as victims of anxiety's relentless grip. Perhaps this fight may call for the assistance of a Christian therapist. If so, that certainly is not a call of shame, but of victory. Anxiety does not have to be a life sentence. Jehoshaphat has some things to teach us about how to deal with extreme situational anxiety.

A Lesson from Jehoshaphat: Oh Jehoshaphat!

Jehoshaphat was the fourth king of Judah around 873 to 848 B.C. He was a good king who accomplished many reforms to help bring the people back to God and do what was right. But even when we seek to do things right, it does not mean we will not experience anxiety. During a time of peace, Jehoshaphat came under sudden attack. In such moments our lives are defined:

> "Some men came and told Jehoshaphat, 'A great multitude is coming against you from Edom, from beyond the sea; and, behold, they are in Hazazon-tamar' (that is, Engedi). Then Jehoshaphat was afraid and set his face to seek the Lord,

> and proclaimed a fast throughout all Judah" (2 Chronicles 20:2-3, ESV).

Jehoshaphat was unprepared for the two armies poised to attack him. I mean, who would be, right? His mind was filled with fear and anxiety when he heard about it. But he did not let his mind stay in that condition.

Seek God First

Fight your fights by going to God first. We learn to stop, drop, and roll when there is a fire. For the Christian, when dire situations arise, we stop, drop, and pray. Jehoshaphat sought God first. He went directly and "set his face" to seek the LORD. He made up his mind that he was not going to focus on the armies, but on the Lord of armies, and he acted on that faith. Jehoshaphat fasted, and he prayed. He prayed about God's character and how He rescued His children in the past.

Faith Over Fear

Fight fear with faith. Then Jehoshaphat stood on the bravery that being one of God's people brings. "If disaster comes upon us, the sword, judgment, or pestilence, or famine, we will stand before this house and before you—for your name is in this house—and cry out to you in our affliction, and you will hear and save" (2 Chronicles 20:9, ESV).

We must stand up to what is provoking us to fear. Reminiscent of Elijah or Daniel or Esther, and other great people of God who stood in the face of fear and held on to the promises and character of God, anxiety was crushed. They defeated anxiety not because they were bigger than their fears and foes, but because their God was. They acted on faith, not fear.

Silencing the "What Ifs"

Fight fear with focus. Key to Jehoshaphat's victory was what came next. Jehoshaphat had his mindset fixed on God. He did not think about the "what ifs" but made up his mind to think about God's promises and boundless capability. Ultimately, what our minds and eyes are fixed upon will determine whether anxiety rules us or we rule it.

What are our eyes fixed upon? Opportunities for anxiety will arise out of nowhere, but we can choose to set our mind and our gaze on Christ instead. Notice I said opportunities. How we view hard places impacts our ability to survive them and even thrive amid them. We need to look at difficulties as opportunities for growth in character and faith.

When We Are Weak, We Are Strong

Fight fear with humility. Pretending we aren't scared is not true bravery. The culture around us tries to combat fear with power. But Scripture says when we are weak, we are strong: "But he said to me, 'My grace is sufficient for you, for my power is made perfect in weakness.' Therefore I will boast all the more gladly about my weaknesses, so that Christ's power may rest on me" (2 Corinthians 12:9, NIV). Jehoshaphat admitted his inability. "O our God, will you not execute judgment on them? For we are powerless against this great horde that is coming against us. We do not know what to do, but our eyes are on you" (2 Chronicles 20:12, ESV).

Christ is our sufficiency for every anxiety or fear we encounter. Mere human strategies will not give us victory. Seeking counsel can help. However, at the end of the day, when we admit our need and ask God to help us, victory is near. As we ourselves battle with anxiety, recognizing its triggers helps us in defeating it.

Fear Is a Liar

Getting rid of fear is a fight. Behind all anxiety is fear of some sort, and truthfully, we are all afraid of something. So, what's the problem with being afraid? It controls and limits us. It holds us back from reaching our potential. Fighting fear like Jehoshaphat did is countercultural. Fighting by surrendering to God, by humbly admitting we are weak, seems counterintuitive. But when we give our fears to God, our God fights for us. The good news is whatever fear we identify with does not have to control us forever. It just means we can now form a battle plan. Below are some common fears that can produce anxiety.

Trigger 1: Fear of Lack

"Fear the Lord, you his holy people, for those who fear him lack nothing" (Psalm 34:9, NIV).

Behind the fear of lack is a sense of being forgotten. Does God see us? Will He provide? Can He be trusted? When we are tempted to panic due to God's provision, it is an invitation to trust in the promises of God.

Time and again I have seen the faithfulness of God meet my family's every need—through job loss, loss of health, loss of what we thought were guarantees in this life. We have received checks in the mail that were unaccounted for and have seen our needs met to the point we could even help others. This is the miracle-working God we serve. God helps those who depend upon Him.

Trigger 2: Fear of Man (Rejection/Popularity)

"Then Saul said to Samuel, 'I have sinned. I violated the LORD's command and your instructions. I was afraid of the men and so I gave in to them'" (1 Samuel 15:24, NIV).

Fear of man can cause us to live for others instead of God. This is a high price to pay. Rejection can become a badge we wear and can cause us to have our relationships become a place of performance as we clamor for acceptance to soothe our anxiety. Looking through the eyes of man's perspective, we will face rejection. Whether we are loved or hated, either can lead us to idolatry. The favor of the Lord is more desirable than man's, who is just a fleeting vapor.

Trigger 3: Fear of Death

"Since the children have flesh and blood, he too shared in their humanity so that by his death he might break the power of him who holds the power of death—that is, the devil—and set free those who all their lives were held in slavery by their fear of death" (Hebrews 2:14-15, NIV).

Fear of death should not be something that plagues (no pun intended) a Christian. Christ took the sting out of death. But if I am honest, at times fear of death has kept me bound as I wanted to keep myself safe to be here for my children. I did not want to die before "my" time, as if I really could control that. But it really is not my time at all. The gift of life is not ours. I know that is hard to wrap our minds around, but when we fear death, we are trying to take control of something only

God controls. He knows the number of our days. Fearing the pain of death disregards the grace of God that will be there in that moment.

We don't need to fear death when we know the Giver of life. Now, I am not saying I want to start skydiving or anything, but the One who walked through the door of death has prepared a place for me and for all who have accepted Christ's gift of salvation. The number of our days might be unknown to us, but it is not unknown to Him. Can we release the anxiety of trying to control our end? Jesus is trustworthy. I know He has carried me through many close calls. None of us will leave this earth one moment before He permits it.

Trigger 4: Fear of Failure

"I sought the Lord, and he answered me; he delivered me from all my fears." (Psalm 34:4, NIV).

Fear of failure can be closely connected with the fear of man. After all, we would not feel shame if we did not have an audience. When we live our lives with a human audience constantly in mind, we will be anxiety-ridden. However, if the measure of success is simply obedience and faithfulness to God, then whatever God wants to do with our work is up to Him. Sticking ourselves out there for possible scrutiny is hard. But when we develop the mentality of looking to God alone for approval, we are freed to reach out to those around us, not hindered by needing other's acceptance.

A huge part of developing as people is failure. Failure is simply a chance to try again. Sometimes what we think is failure is really only comparing ourselves to someone else. We only fail if we stop trying. Failure is a closed door that God allowed. It does not define our worth. Unfortunately, we will have to slay this dragon of fear of failure many times as we remember not to define our success by man's measure.

Trigger 5: Fear of Being You

"For we are his workmanship, created in Christ Jesus for good works, which God prepared beforehand, that we should walk in them" (Ephesians 2:10, ESV).

Supposedly one of the greatest fears is speaking in front of people. Frankly, this comes from a place of insecurity and the pursuit of acceptance from man. Behind the door of this fear is shame once again. The enemy uses this insidious tool to silence his victims so they will be overcome with anxiety, too afraid to do anything. Our willingness to admit our weakness could be the very thing that helps people hope in God. God begins and completes the work in us. The pressure is off us to be anything other than what God made us to be.

Be you. There is truly no other you in this world. Your unique story with Jesus is what people need to see. As we pour out our inability, God fills us with His ability. He's such a faithful God. When we abandon this fear, we are suddenly able to focus on meeting the needs of others rather than worrying about our appearance or performance.

So, friends, I certainly am not a perfect example of living without fear. I am OK with that. We will not live perfectly while on this earth. But if we stay close to our Savior, He will help us navigate all the fears that threaten our heart and make us stagnant in our faith. How beautiful it is when fear leads us to the comforting arms of God. Fear is the common denominator of all the different forms of anxiety. We can let it go.

Be Brave

The world needs us to be brave. It needs to see people who live out their faith and step out of themselves onto the "water" of God's enablement. We don't have to display a fake bravery but an authentic one that admits our fears and moves forward anyway. Ultimately, there is One alone whom we should fear. Solomon sought after the answer to the meaning of life and found it was simply this: "Having heard everything, I have reached this conclusion: Fear God and keep his commandments, because this is the whole duty of man" (Ecclesiastes 12:13, NET). Replacing our many fears with one right fear gives us peace.

How We Stop Being Anxious and Find Peace

We have a heritage in Christ. We have a solution to the multitude of anxieties that can plague us, just as the psalmist did. God is our comfort. We can choose peace over anxiety as it says in Colossians: "Let the peace of Christ be in control in your heart (for you were in fact called as one body to this peace), and be thankful" (Colossians 3:15, NET). We were called to have peace.

The peace of Christ can control our thinking. But how? By making up our mind. The word "let" is revealing. We already have peace that Christ gave us. Why aren't we using His peace? We have not let it. Christ's peace controls our thinking when we, by faith, think about what God tells us to think about. The enemy will make us feel like we cannot, but friend, again, God wouldn't say we could if we couldn't. Paul has some tips to offer us in dealing with anxiety.

Tip 1: Being In Christ

Whatever form of anxiety we may encounter, it can feel inescapable. Why does it happen to us? Is it something we can change? Being in Christ has benefits that often go beyond our realization. On one hand we can forfeit the grace that is ours and the peace that Christ gives. However, Paul teaches we can claim the benefit of peace if we are willing to live by God's principles:

> "Don't worry about anything; instead, pray about everything. Tell God what you need, and thank him for all he has done. Then you will experience God's peace, which exceeds anything we can understand. His peace will guard your hearts and minds as you live in Christ Jesus." (Philippians 4:6-7, NLT).

The passage above starts with familiar words. They remind me of the song, "Don't Worry, Be Happy." I love that song but really dislike the simplicity of that phrase. IT IS NOT THAT EASY. Or is it?

Paul certainly experienced anxiety through his beatings, imprisonments, shipwrecks, stonings, persecutions. I would say he is an authority on the subject. Living into the reality of being in Christ gave Paul power to overcome. A relationship with God is the difference between living in anxiety or living in Christ.

Tip 2: Humility—Going on the Offensive and Defensive

Paul invites us to take an offensive and defensive approach in Philippians 4:6-7.

Offensive approach: We come to God for help and prepare our mind. In humility, we admit our need (verse 6). It takes guts and humility to admit we are anxious or concerned about something. It means we know we cannot handle it on our own. The world around us does not want to give credit to anyone besides self and can view faith as a crutch. But the One who created us knows best. Humility heals us while pride kills us. Admitting we need help is what leads to our rescue.

Defensive approach: We don't just stay there; we do something. We pray. Hard. We cry out. We move away from anxiety by moving toward Jesus and His Word. God did not create us to be independent but dependent upon Him in a beautiful relationship. We were never supposed to be enough on our own.

Tip 3: Stop Whining

Gratitude is an elixir that causes joy to bubble up (Philippians 4:6). Yes, even gratitude for that thorn in our flesh has a way of giving us perspective, taking our eyes off self, and putting it on the One who is over every struggle we face. Genuine gratitude is not fake or religious. It searches for the goodness of God right smack dab in the middle of the hard and understands just how crazy blessed we are. The creation was never supposed to be our joy. Creator God is.

Tip 4: Fix Our Thoughts

While our thoughts can be overwhelming at times, especially when we are burdened with emotional turmoil, the truth is we are in control of our thoughts. We can fix our thoughts on what we want to think about. "Therefore, holy brothers and sisters, who share in the heavenly calling, fix your thoughts on Jesus, whom we acknowledge as our apostle and high priest" (Hebrews 3:1, NIV). This will require kicking out negative thinking and replacing it with thinking on our Savior. Sometimes this will call for a major fight requiring a full-on defensive approach, too.

Tip 5: Get Up and Fight—Strategic Tactics

The best way to fight fear, the dominant emotion behind anxiety, is with faith. We must cling to God's promises to be victorious. It will be a fight. Here are a few tactics that have helped me.

Embrace the power of God. "For God has not given us a spirit of fear, but of power and of love and of a sound mind" (2 Timothy 1:7, NKJV). If God hasn't given us fear, who has? It is either us or the enemy of our souls. Remember God is all-powerful. He is well able to give us what we need and to help us to overcome. Notice, I did not say *we* are able, but *He* is as we rely on Him. We can let go of fear and anxiety.

Choose the mind of Christ. For those of us who are Christians, we already have the mind of Christ. "'For who has understood the mind of the LORD so as to instruct Him?' But we have the mind of Christ" (1 Corinthians 2:16, ESV). Taking God at His Word, we silence the thoughts that don't line up with His truth. To debunk the myths pumping through the media and our brains, we need be well-acquainted with His truth.

Choose mind renewal. We can renew our minds! "Do not conform to the pattern of this world, but be transformed by the renewing of your mind. Then you will be able to test and approve what God's will is—his good, pleasing and perfect will" (Romans 12:2, NIV). This is not a passive activity. We must "suit up" to face the battles of the mind, form a battle plan, and enlist accountability. Memorizing Scripture, reflecting on it, reading, and studying it daily with a Bible reading plan nourishes our spirit and strengthens us for the fight.

Recognize our spiritual wealth in Christ. We have it all. "His divine power has given us everything we need for a godly life through our knowledge of him who called us by his own glory and goodness" (2 Peter 1:3, NIV). We don't know how blessed we really are. The deceiver has blinded our eyes and distracted us with troubles. We walk through a minefield daily, but God's Word guides us through every single ambush we face. Through knowing Him, His character, and His Word, we always know His intentions and purposes are for our good and His glory. The enemy wins if he can get us to doubt God's goodness. But why would we believe the evil one over the One who will never fail us?

Freedom Is a Choice

In the end, freedom in our minds is a choice. One person can be in prison, yet free. Another person can be physically free yet imprisoned in one's own mind. Freedom from fear or anxiety does not come from our circumstances but from God's Word. So many thoughts flow through our minds. These thoughts influence us and sometimes become a part of our mindset, making it hard to shake negative thoughts and adopt the mind of Christ.

Getting to the Root

Sometimes a mindset can become a default in certain situations, and we just accept it as how we deal with or process things. But mindsets are not a life sentence. We can learn how to handle things differently. Jesus showed us the key to overcoming anxiety.

Mindset of Christ

As our Savior prayed in the Garden of Gethsemane, He experienced a medical condition called *hematidrosis*, where He sweat blood. This condition was not a sign of lack of faith on His part but a physical response to the immense stress He was under. God Incarnate felt the same grief and anxiety we do, and He chose to feel it rather than avoid it.

Christ told His disciples to be with Him while He faced intense stress. He knew the suffering that was about to be inflicted upon Him. "Then he said to them, 'My soul is overwhelmed with sorrow to the point of death. Stay here and keep watch with me'" (Matthew 26:38, NIV). Contrast this with how we often don't know what is coming but fear things that might not ever happen.

As the time drew near for His suffering, Christ did not seek a way out but surrendered to the Father's will to be done. What do we do when we feel overwhelmed? When we seek to control our circumstances, we typically become more overwhelmed. But when we choose to trust God and lay down our will and way in the face of fear, we overcome. Jesus demonstrated how powerful surrender can be as He fixed His mind on God's will and not His own.

Mind Renewal: Keys to Unlock Our Mind

Key Thought:

The peace of Christ can guard our hearts and minds in Christ Jesus when we yield control and our will to God.

Key Verse:

"You keep him in perfect peace whose mind is stayed on you, because he trusts in you" (Isaiah 26:3, ESV).

Key Change: Application—Releasing Fear and Choosing Faith

Fear is a powerful emotion. It feels like a foe that cannot be defeated. But we can be sure if God told us not to fear over 400 times in Scripture, it must be possible. We can make up our mind to choose faith over fear and strength over anxiety through Christ who is our strength.

Counselor's Corner

Thinking courageous thoughts takes practice and a change of word choice. "I can't" when changed to "I might be able to" opens the possibility of what a God who is bigger than us can do in and through us. I have found three little words to be game changers for me and my clients: "with God's help." When God called me to write, I almost laughed. Running a counseling center and raising kids with a husband who travels seemed more than this fun-loving woman could juggle. But with God's help, deadlines have been met, and books have been published. Leaving room for "with God's help" can empower us to face our past, give us the courage to try something new, or even energize us to chase dreams that feel beyond reach.

When counseling children, I teach them that giving into their feelings of fear can grow a "worry dragon" that seems bigger than them. I confidently tell them that in over 20 years, "I've never met a worry dragon bigger than God." How about you? What thoughts can you think and what steps of courage can you take to shrink the worry dragon in your life? Worries about our children's futures, finances, relationships, and our own health, when allowed to circulate over and over in our minds, will cause tension in our bodies, drain our energy, and lead to panic disorders. Every time we grab ahold of an anxious thought and take it captive (2 Corinthians 10:5), replacing it with words of reassurance and hope that God is for us (Romans 8:31), we shrink our worry dragon. Courageous thoughts replace anxious worries as we retrain our brains thought by thought, day by day, and week by week.

When working with Christian clients, I bring God into the picture with an empowering activity they can use to practice new thoughts. This intervention is not meant to cause them to ignore reality but rather to acknowledge their feelings with "even though" statements. I then ask them to bring God into the picture.

- Even though I am scared, I know God is for me.
- Even though I think no one will want to talk to me, I am trusting God to help me make friends.
- Even though I want to quit, I know God will not fail me.
- Even though I don't think I can do it, I am trying anyway and counting on God to fill in the gaps.
- Even though I don't want to, I am trusting God to change my heart.

I hope you will try this right now. Think of something that scares you, intimidates you, or causes you discomfort. After acknowledging how you feel with an "even though" clause, create an "I am" statement that incorporates God to empower you with new confidence. Then say those words out loud, which gives them more power and crowds out other thoughts. Bringing God into the picture of our lives transforms our thoughts, feelings and ultimately our behaviors.

Sometimes my clients struggle with creating these statements because the negativity of their thoughts and intensity of their emotions seems locked in their brains. They often wish for a faster cure that doesn't require the intense energy and effort required for this practice to work. Unfortunately, anxious thinking almost always begins in childhood, forming those neuropathways for decades. While words probably won't instantaneously erase our fear, they can shrink the anxiety to the point that we can reach out for God's hand (Isaiah 41:10) and act in faith knowing God is with us (John 1:14). Over time, our brain's muscle memory will kick in, and the exercise will become more natural.

I pray for my clients as they are fighting to regain control over their thoughts and emotions. I also encourage them to reach out to a few trusted friends asking them to pray for them specifically, get on their church prayer list, or join a small group asking for prayer. Mindset battles are also spiritual battles.

Mindset Movement 1: *Start incorporating "with God's help" and "even though" statements into your thoughts and speech.*

Mindset Movement 2: *Seek out prayer support to assist you in fighting your mindset battles.*

Chapter Four

The Depressive Mindset—Battling Discouragement and Disillusionment

"I waited patiently for the LORD; he turned to me and heard my cry. He lifted me out of the slimy pit, out of the mud and mire; he set my feet upon a rock and gave me a firm place to stand. He put a new song in my mouth, a hymn of praise to our God."

—Psalm 40:1-3a, NIV

Life is hard sometimes. Real hard. And yes, it is OK for Christians to admit that. Not to admit it would be a lie after all. Other people's highlight reels scream at us that we are not measuring up to their level of happiness. Maybe we scramble to show others we are just as happy if not happier than they are, or maybe we just sink into sad thoughts about our current condition. Deep down we wonder about the madness of life and if we are really as happy as we should be.

But what if it's our mind that determines our happiness? What if it's our choices, not somebody else's, that affect us most? And what if joy or happiness, whatever it's called, is the heritage for all who are in Christ Jesus, regardless of our circumstances? Walking in the spiritual reality of joy might take some time and perseverance to learn. But it is possible. It will just require rewiring our mindset to understand what real joy is.

Finding Our Way to Happiness

Abraham Lincoln put it rather succinctly: "People are about as happy as they make up their mind to be."[10] However, at times there are some hurdles in the way to be sure. If we have a problem and admit it (the first step), there is an app for that. Or a pill. There is always some potential remedy that may treat our symptoms so we can get back to normal again. It's OK to have problems—they're not fun, but part of life. Problems are part of the new normal in a world operating under the curse.

It's also OK to not be OK. Jesus promised us problems, not perfection. "I have told you these things, so that in me you may have peace. In this world you will have trouble. But take heart! I have overcome the world" (John 16:33, NIV). Jesus gave us a heads-up about the harsh realities of life here on earth—not to discourage us but to warn and prepare us. But Jesus also reassured us that amid His clear-eyed prediction of anticipated suffering there would also be the reality of His victory and His presence.

The facade of the perfect life is perhaps also the impetus for the depressed mindset. There is no perfect life on this earth. And deep within our souls is this cavity of emptiness that longs for eternity. It was put there by God (Ecclesiastes

3:11). Why? So we would search for Him and find our contentment and joy in Him alone.

Nothing of this earth will satisfy us like the One who made us. This being our reality, while we try to navigate this fallen world we will, from time to time, encounter a depressive mindset. And friends, it is hard. It is, like the other mindsets, within our own mind and difficult to figure a way out of. It's difficult, but not impossible.

Depressive Mindset Versus Clinical Depression

Depression diagnoses can be handed out without much fanfare. If you are sad, it might be depression. If you are tired, it might be depression. If you are moody, it might be … you get it. But true depression differs from the episodic depressive mindset that most everyone will experience at some point in life. Whether it is the "baby blues," situational discouragement, hormonally related erratic emotions, a melancholic personality, or simply in the DNA, a depressive mindset seems impossible to overcome. Like other negative mindsets, the depressive mindset is a lens we view life through that colors our perspective with hues of discouragement or disillusionment.

In this chapter we will focus on the depressive mindset common to us all, and at the end of the chapter, counselor Michelle Nietert will share some insights to help with both the depressive mindset as well as clinical depression.

Identifying the Problem

No one wants to be classified as depressed. People can cast all kinds of judgment for such a diagnosis. But the truth is, we cannot find a solution if we do not first identify the problem. The depressive mindset does not happen overnight unless it is brought on by a traumatic event. However, even then, it is our response to the event that determines whether our mindset will be changed by it.

Little by little we can acquiesce to a vicious depressive mindset that takes the joy out of living. Moods don't change with the flick of the switch, but we can learn how to guide the mood we are having by renewing our mind. Experts across the spectrum say that depression doesn't just happen because of the level of brain chemicals one has. Genetics, stressful circumstances, medications, mood swings, and medical problems also can play a role in depression.

I would add to this that the chief cause of a depressive mindset is spiritual. Therefore, the solution is also spiritual. In some cases, medication might be a part of the solution, but sometimes medication can mask the real problem. Whereas, if we allow ourselves to process the lows and highs of life with God's Word, we can work through what seems impossible.

Several years back I went to visit one of my daughters. During that trip she wept profusely, desperate for answers: "Mom, I am depressed. I have been depressed for over six years, and I don't know how to get out. Why has God allowed this to happen to me?"

I wept with her and held her so tightly in that moment. I knew she had been struggling with depression. My heart ached that I could not fix her problem. Unlike the Band-Aids and a kiss that could fix physical problems when she was younger, this problem in the mind seemed impossible and out of reach.

"I don't know, Sweetheart," I said. "But I do know God is not going to leave you in that place of depression. That is not in His character. I know He is going to use this in your life. Because of this, you will be able to help many. I believe you will have victory in this area of your life very soon."

My daughter, who holds a degree in psychology, is fierce in her faith, and she readily admits when she is struggling with issues in her mind. But like the psalmist in Psalm 40, she did not let it define her. She admitted her need and her struggle as she fought for deliverance.

Sometimes we just need to know how to fight. She fought on her knees. She saturated her mind in God's words, not her own. She became aware of the need to take captive thoughts that were negative and to speak truth to them. She cried out for help. She worshiped God right in the middle of the pain. And she won. But it was a long, hard fight.

Many of the principles that helped her to win that battle are in this chapter. We all can win, too, friends. We just have to fight with the right tools, which will be shared in this chapter. And we can't give up. We only lose the battle of the mind if we stop fighting.

Numbness Is Not a Solution

Sometimes to avoid the pain of a depressive mindset, we can succumb to feeling numb. If we don't like our reality, it seems easier to pretend it is different or to avoid feeling altogether. We live in a culture where crying is seen as a bad thing, so we hold in or suppress our emotions. But they will come out at some point. And when they do, it isn't going to be pretty. Can you say, big, ugly cry?

During one season of struggling against a depressive mindset, I ached to get out of it but did not know how. Then I came across a book titled *How to Cry Out to God*. I can't find that book now, but God had it for me when I needed it. This book taught me that instead of giving in to our feelings, we should instruct them. We don't need to fight the feeling itself, rather we can push through the feeling to where we are close enough to Jesus to grab the hem of His robe. We can show God our feelings and even cry out loud if needed, grabbing His Word and promises as if they are our very life.

When we don't know what to say, the Holy Spirit will help us: "In the same way, the Spirit helps us in our weakness. We do not know what we ought to pray for, but the Spirit himself intercedes for us through wordless groans. And he who searches our hearts knows the mind of the Spirit, because the Spirit intercedes for God's people in accordance with the will of God" (Romans 8:26-27, NIV). The Holy Spirit knows the mind of the Spirit. God already knows what we need before we ask Him. It's not healthy to stifle our emotions, and we will not find victory until we are ready to face them. How we face them makes all the difference.

Releasing the Stigma

Shame rising from our struggle with a depressive mindset can hinder our recovery from it. Those of us struggling with sadness, discouragement, disillusionment, even depression must let go of the stigma. A depressive mindset is part of the human condition. We are in good company with those who have encountered the depressive mindset and have overcome—King David, Jeremiah, Job, to name a few.

To defend ourselves against the stigma that depression invites, it is important to find support from people who will encourage us in Christ rather than slam us for struggling because "Christians are not supposed to struggle with depression." We can release the stigma because Christ showed us how. "… Looking to Jesus, the founder and perfecter of our faith, who for the joy that was set before him endured the cross, despising the shame, and is seated at the right hand of the throne of God" (Hebrews 12:2, ESV). Christ did not allow shame and suffering to stop Him. We don't have to either. Hope is the antidote to a depressive mindset. Jeremiah revealed how one can have hope even during great suffering.

A Lesson from Jeremiah: The Weeping Prophet

With a nickname like "the weeping prophet," Jeremiah is an easy pick for someone who battled with a depressive mindset. He even wrote the book of Lamentations. Called by God to speak to a people who would not listen, Jeremiah's task felt impossible. It was a discouraging assignment that cultivated mental anguish and disillusionment.

Sometimes we think God's calling should translate into easy times. However, it is often hard times that shape us into the calling of God. In the middle of hardship Jeremiah told God's people there was always hope:

> "For I know the plans I have for you, declares the LORD, plans for welfare and not for evil, to give

> you a future and a hope. Then you will call upon me and come and pray to me, and I will hear you. You will seek me and find me, when you seek me with all your heart" (Jeremiah 29:11-13, ESV).

God called Jeremiah to speak hope and encouragement to the Israelites during their time of captivity. This was no easy task since Jeremiah's message came as the proverbial sky was falling, and he stood holding only an umbrella of hope promising that times would be better. The people did not appreciate his message. They persecuted him and wanted to kill him.

The hope God promised through Jeremiah was not immediate, but it was a promise. God's hope is certain, and He has a good end in mind. God's people access this hope simply by faith in the God who promises it. As we seek God, we will find a hope that never ends, no matter what is going on around us.

Jeremiah, who spoke about this hope, also had his own moments of doubt and uncertainty. However, he talked with God about it. He did not turn away from God but toward Him, crying out:

> "O LORD, you know; remember me and visit me, and take vengeance for me on my persecutors. In your forbearance take me not away; know that for your sake I bear reproach. Your words were found, and I ate them, and your words became to me a joy and the delight of my heart, for I am called by your name, O LORD, God of hosts" (Jeremiah 15:15-16, ESV).

There is a peace in knowing that God knows. Nothing escapes His view. His timing and perspective are different than ours, but perfect. It was eating God's Word that gave Jeremiah joy. Right in the middle of a depressive mindset, Jeremiah received joy, fueled by hope. The Hebrew word for "ate" means to devour, consume, feed upon. This does not describe a passive reading of God's Word but an ingesting of it. Jeremiah hunted through God's Word for hope and life and sustenance for his very soul in the worst of times.

God's calling is not easy. Part of living through the human condition means we will encounter mental anguish like Jeremiah did. And David did. And Jesus did. On we could go. The Word of God was the refuge of each of these people. It can be ours, too. But it will require more than a casual read. We cannot escape mental pain in this life, but we can learn how to walk through it victoriously and choose joy.

The Depressive Mindset: Not Just an Emotion

Depression is an overused word today in a society immersed in self. But the depressive mindset is more than an emotion. It is an attack on our souls and a battle for hope and joy.

Sometimes we feel a need to be "true to our feelings," but our feelings are not true to us. Feelings are not facts. It's time for us to suit up and examine our emotions in light of what God says. We don't have to give in to the sad feelings. We have a choice: let ourselves be tortured by our emotions or rule them. Here are just a few of the stumbling blocks that try to keep us bound in a depressive mindset.

Trigger 1: Feelings Aren't Facts

Just because we think a thought doesn't make it true. Sad thoughts can pull us in. We feel sorry for ourselves. The sadness seems justified. But if we are not careful, those thoughts will not just carry us away; they will bury us. We must take our thoughts captive to test them and see if they are true. The problem is even our own hearts are deceitful. We cannot trust our own mind. Oh, how much we need God!

Even when our feelings are valid, we do not have to give ourselves over to them. We can feel sorrow, but then we can also bring our sorrow to God, which helps us turn the sorrow into dancing: "You have turned my mourning into joyful dancing. You have taken away my clothes of mourning and clothed me with joy" (Psalm 30:11, NLT).

When we bring our thoughts to God and use His Word as a lens to help us see truth, we heal. But we must remove all doubt about God's Word being the final authority. What God's Word says about us triumphs over what our own minds or others have to say about us. God is the authority, and He is not a man that He should lie (Numbers 23:19).

Trigger 2: Expect the Unexpected

Peter knew all about unexpected troubles. Perhaps many of us feel like experts on this topic as well. Just when we get comfortable, the other shoe drops, right? Where is God in all of this? He is with us.

We tend to expect a trouble-free life and are shocked when life is hard. This creates disillusionment as what we expected does not come to fruition. Sometimes this happens because our expectations have become idols that need to be laid down. Peter challenges us to think of our trials differently:

> "Beloved, do not be surprised at the fiery ordeal among you, which comes upon you for your testing, as though something strange were happening to you; but to the degree that you share the sufferings of Christ, keep on rejoicing, so that at the revelation of His glory you may also rejoice and be overjoyed" (1 Peter 4:12-13, NASB).

Why shouldn't we be surprised? God did not promise a perfect life. "I have told you these things, so that in me you may have peace. In this world you will have trouble. But take heart! I have overcome the world" (John 16:33, NIV). Still, we tend to set our compass toward perfection, which is not what a fallen world can deliver.

There is sorrow in letting go of our ideal, but it wasn't ours in the first place. Every trial is an opportunity to be on mission for Jesus. When life is hard, when we remove the focus from self, we will not be dragged down in a depressive mindset.

Peter even suggests we rejoice in our sufferings. This is a mindset change for sure, right? While this probably feels impossible, this is the abundant life Christ promised. When we accept God's culture instead of man's, our joy returns. Our hope should not be for a perfect life, but that the perfect One will be with us in whatever this life brings, the expected or unexpected.

Trigger 3: Disillusionment is an Illusion

When the unexpected happens and we suffer profound loss, disillusionment can cause us to doubt God. In our mind, life was not supposed to look like it does. Now what? Our feelings seem inescapable, as if we are obligated to give into them.

But feelings are illusions, friends. They are works of imagination we can turn into a better reality.

We can direct our thoughts. Let's say it together: "We can direct our thoughts through Christ." Thoughts focused on what should have been—sad thoughts, bad thoughts—can be changed as we walk in the Spirit. "For to set the mind on the flesh is death, but to set the mind on the Spirit is life and peace" (Romans 8:6, ESV).

Regurgitating the hopelessness of this world will keep us bound in grief. Sad thoughts are not the reality of the inheritance we have in Christ. We have a hope vastly superior to anything this world can give us. We can set our mind on this reality and ask God to help us let go of thoughts that pull us down.

Trigger 4: Counterfeit Joy

Sometimes we give in to a depressive mindset because we hoped in a counterfeit joy. This means we looked for life in something created rather than in the Creator, who is the source of lasting joy. Joy is not something we can buy or something we can own. It is something we access as we seek Christ.

Paul reminded us of the source of joy, hope, and peace. And we access this joy by believing He can give it: "May the God of hope fill you with all joy and peace in believing, so that by the power of the Holy Spirit you may abound in hope" (Romans 15:13, ESV). So even though this might seem like an obvious question, have we asked God to release us from a depressive mindset? Sometimes we have not because we ask not. We must persevere in faith in our requests to God: "Until now you have asked nothing in my name. Ask, and you will receive, that your joy may be full" (John 16:24, ESV).

We are to ask so that our joy may be full. This doesn't say our emotions will be full, and there will be no problems. Remember, Jesus had joy even as He carried the cross on the way to His crucifixion. This joy is not shallow or superficial. It is deep, embedded in the grace of God, and filled to overflowing by the Holy Spirit.

The Path to Victory

In Psalm 40, the psalmist felt his depression intensely. He offered some lessons to those who join him in the pit of depression. The psalmist made some hard choices. He chose to be patient. He chose to call out to God. He chose to believe God and not his feelings. He chose to worship. Such worship truly is a sacrifice of praise: "I waited patiently for the Lord; he turned to me and heard my cry. He lifted me out of the slimy pit, out of the mud and mire; he set my feet on a rock and gave me a firm place to stand. He put a new song in my mouth, a hymn of praise to our God" (Psalm 40:1-3a, NIV).

Choosing Joy

We all want to be happy, joyful to overflowing. But it is easy to believe the lie that instead of joy coming from an active choice, it is an emotion that happens to the lucky ones. Confronting this lie was the significant key that helped my daughter unlock true joy and ditch depression. After six years of fighting depression, she found her victory. This did not mean she would not face the depressive mindset again, but it meant she knew how to put it in its place and out of her mind.

During worship leading with my daughters at a women's conference, the Holy Spirit nudged me to ask my daughter to share her testimony about the victory God gave her over depression. Normally my daughter would profess shyness at such a suggestion, but in the Spirit, she knew she was being called to share. As she described her struggle and process to overcome the depression, a hush fell over the entire room. Women wept. Women prayed. Stirred to admit their need, they chose to do a daring thing. They claimed, "If God can do it for her, He can do it for me!"

To this day, a group from that church still meets to encourage one another and share the victory from depression that they, too, experienced that day. Christ promised us an abundant life full of joy. The enemy wants to steal that away from us, but we don't have to let him do it. We can choose joy. Here's how.

Tip 1: Hope

The very message Jeremiah was charged to tell the people of God was a word he had to apply when facing the depressive mindset: hope. David had to apply hope in his life as well: "Why am I discouraged? Why is my heart so sad? I will put my hope in God! I will praise him again—my Savior and my God!" (Psalm 42:11, NLT). Hope was the prescription that healed David when his soul was giving in to the depressive mindset. Hope is not something we just do with our mind, but it starts there. We can choose in what—or in whom—we hope.

In the Psalm above David said, "I *will* put my hope in God." It was a choice. Hoping for a perfect life is not real hope. Hoping in better circumstances is not hope. Hoping in Christ means we believe what He said about our future. That means our present reality will not always be, and God is always enough to get us through today.

Tip 2: Remember

Jeremiah lost sight of happiness: "My soul has been excluded from peace; I have forgotten happiness" (Lamentations 3:17, NASB). But he found happiness again by remembering:

> "But this I call to mind, and therefore I have hope: The steadfast love of the LORD never ceases; his mercies never come to an end; they are new every morning; great is your faithfulness. 'The LORD is my portion,' says my soul, 'therefore I will hope in him'" (Lamentations 3:21-24, ESV).

How do we communicate about our depressive mindset? Jeremiah was used by God to write what he was experiencing, his authentic heart cry, in the books of Jeremiah and Lamentations. We've all seen the social media posts that show a soul overcome with the depressive mindset. So often we can vent on social media or complain to others who cannot truly help us.

Depressive thoughts can be overwhelming. We can feel a relentless hopeless message pumping through our brains so strongly. But just like Jeremiah did, we can call to mind other thoughts that move us from the depressive mindset. When we communicate words of life, we inform our minds instead of our minds informing us. Rather than reflecting on all the sad things, when we look to our Redeemer and remember all God has done throughout history, we know we will not be forgotten. When we cast our cares on Him, there is always hope.

Tip 3: Let Christ Be Our Comfort

Nothing in this world can ultimately comfort us. Not for long, anyway. We were made for another world. When we keep going to the dry well of this world for refreshment, we will find ourselves empty. God is near, friends, when we are hurting. "The Lord is close to the brokenhearted and saves those who are crushed in spirit" (Psalm 34:18, NIV).

A depressive mindset is a crushed spirit, and a crushed spirit is a spiritual matter. Christ is our help and hope for spiritual matters. Christ's nearness is a refuge and a comfort when sadness looms large. In Psalm 16, David shows us how to exercise our faith to find this illusive joy. It is found in God's presence: "You make known to me the path of life; you will fill me with joy in your presence, with eternal pleasures at your right hand" (Psalm 16:11, ESV).

We can cognitively know this, but experiencing it is another thing. God's presence is not casually entered. We enter God's presence through worship. Sometimes when in the depressive mindset, worshiping God means giving Him a sacrifice of praise. It may be all we can do is weep in His presence. But if we can just seek Him and give thanks to Him for all He has done, that is enough. We can immerse our mind in His Word, turn down the noise of the world, and just be. We don't have to let our problems dictate our moods. We can bring our problems to Jesus and choose to let Him comfort us. The absence of trouble is not where joy is found. The presence of God is.

Tip 4: Get Busy

God still has plans for us, friends. We can find our purpose and stay on mission. Depressive mindset or not, it will be a hard fight. But we don't have to give in to it. What we focus on determines our victory. When we give in to the depressive mindset, we become self-focused.

Our mind becomes like a labyrinth, full of thoughts that do not edify us or encourage joy. Sometimes just being busy about the things of God can help resolve depression. This doesn't mean avoiding our pain and busying ourselves to bury ourselves. But when we change our focus to serving others instead of ourselves, we tap into a natural joy that helps us see our problems in focus with reality.

We Are Seen

Sitting a bowshot away from her son, Hagar could not bear to watch him suffer. She cried out. And. God. Saw. Her. One of the lies behind the depressive mindset is that we are not seen. No one understands. But the truth is we never escape God's view, and He catches every tear we cry: "You keep track of all my sorrows. You have collected all my tears in your bottle. You have recorded each one in your book" (Psalm 56:8, NLT).

Sometimes we just want the pain to go away. If God sees us, why doesn't He do something about it? But the God who sees is doing more than we know. And He promises to use all things together for our good and His glory (Romans 8:28). Do we trust Him? Hagar, a slave on the run, did. Just knowing God saw her was enough. And then He provided.

God sees us, too, friends. He sees the sadness of our soul. And He wants to meet us in that pit. As Corrie Ten Boom once said, "There is no pit so deep, that God's love is not deeper still."[11] God saw Corrie when she was in a Nazi concentration camp. He saw Hagar in the desert. He sees us right where we are. And He is with us. This is the secret inner joy we have. Our God is with us through it all. We can let Him fill that void.

Getting to the Root

At the root of the depressive mindset is the feeling of hopelessness. We feel forgotten, and there is no solution. We are not seen. We are not cherished. No one cares. But don't believe those lies. That's what they are. We can turn to the promises of God and remember His goodness. When life is hard, He is an ever-present help in times of trouble. And Christ showed us how to endure when we face the depressive mindset.

Mindset of Christ

"He was despised and rejected by men, a man of sorrows and acquainted with grief; and as one from whom men hide their faces he was despised, and we esteemed him not" (Isaiah 53:3, ESV). Christ knew what it was to be hated and rejected—even by those He had created and died for. And He knew what it was to battle the depressive mindset. Though the root to the word "sorrows" in the expression "man of sorrows" literally means pain, and is used to "express physical suffering, it much more commonly has to do with mental anguish."[12]

Christ did not have to suffer mentally, but He chose to. He chose to become the Son of Man to identify with our weaknesses so He could show us the way to victory. He did not give in to the sorrow. We don't have to either.

Christ endured. He patiently put up with all His own people did to Him. "Consider him who endured such opposition from sinners, so that you will not grow weary and lose heart"

(Hebrews 12:3, NIV). He kept Himself busy with God's work. "I must work the works of Him that sent me, while it is day; the night is coming, when no one can work" (John 9:4, NKJV). He stayed on mission and did not look for joy in this life. His joy was doing the will of the Father.

Mind Renewal: Keys to Unlock Our Mind

Key Thought:

A depressive mind does not have to be a life sentence. Choose joy.

Key Verse: Truth from God's Word

"Though you have not seen him, you love him. Though you do not now see him, you believe in him and rejoice with joy that is inexpressible and filled with glory" (1 Peter 1:8, ESV).

Key Change: Application—Release Sadness and Hunt for Joy

Search and find reasons to celebrate in your life. Cultivate real gratitude (not fake positivity, yuck!), and get your eyes off the things that pull you down. Journal about what you are grateful for and search for Scriptures that speak truth about the hope and joy we have in Christ.

Counselor's Corner

"Hope deferred makes the heart sick ..." (Proverbs 13:12a, NIV). Think about what this verse means. When hope is deferred—meaning life doesn't turn out the way we hoped or planned and we believe this pattern will continue—our heart (and mind) can become sick, sad, stuck, or depressed.

Depression can occur slowly, especially when sadness and anger aren't addressed and get stuck in our bodies. Our energy levels drop. We work to survive each day, showing little interest in the things we used to love and focusing more on what's wrong with ourselves and our world than what's right. We struggle to fall asleep and stay asleep. This pattern can manifest itself as depression, a leading cause of disability in the world (WHO, 2020).[13]

If you are currently struggling with depression, you are not alone. If left untreated, depression can cycle in and out of our lives for years, robbing us of our ability to experience hope and joy. Treating depression involves a wholistic approach where mental health professionals often work with other healthcare providers addressing our client's physical, psychological, relational, and spiritual needs.

The first step to changing your negative thoughts is to track them. Writing on paper your innermost thoughts helps you to examine them. I do an exercise with clients in which they take a sheet of paper, fold it in half, and write their negative thoughts on the left-hand side. Next, I ask them to work through a series of questions attempting to be a neutral observer of their own life;

"Is it true?"

"Am I sure it's true?"

"What if it's not true?"

"What if the opposite is true?"

On the right side, I ask them to write a positive truth based on Scripture they would like to believe instead. This helps them see the contrast between the two and gives them a tangible tool for overcoming negativity.

During this exercise I also ask clients to use "I am" statements whenever possible, which helps them separate performance from personhood. If people can't fully embrace the truth contained in the Scriptures they referenced, sometimes they can take a baby step by repeating the following: "I am learning or beginning to believe … " before reciting the positive truth based on Scripture.

Next, comes the part that makes the lasting difference. We use a timer to track how long it takes to write or say the "I am" statements. Realizing this assignment will only take a few minutes helps the client see that they have time in their day for this activity. The clients then plan when and where they will practice their declarations daily. With the onset of telehealth counseling, my clients and I can even locate the space in their home they will use to practice new mindsets. Using sticky notes and placing them in often seen locations—bathroom mirrors, car steering wheels, kitchen sinks—reinforces the practice of daily reprogramming their brain. Practicing positive "I am" statements based on God's Word a few minutes a day creates lasting transformation.

Physical interventions are important, too. Most of us have heard that energy produces more energy. Let's see if you can create additional energy at this very moment. Set down your book and move both arms up and down like doing a jumping jack. Do you feel a little more energy in your body? When we are depressed moving is the last thing we *feel* like doing, but creating small movements can lead to positive change.

Research still validates that exercising or moving 20-30 minutes, five times a week, has the same impact on our bodies as a low-dose antidepressant.[14] Movement lowers stress hormones, and bilateral movement like walking can reinforce cognitive change in the body and brain. It's so effective I even tell my clients who are struggling with movement to bring their walking shoes, and we walk while we do talk therapy. By the end of our session, they experience for themselves how movement impacts energy levels and sense of emotional well-being.

Consulting a doctor is important when addressing physical contributions to depression. Vitamin D levels, hormones, blood sugar, and thyroid issues should be checked regularly. My clients who progress the fastest usually approach their depression not only by attending counseling on a regular basis, but also by seeking the help of a doctor and sometimes additional healthcare professionals, like a nutritionist and physical therapist. Using a team of healthcare professionals empowers people struggling with mental health issues to create faster, longer lasting change.

One of my favorite modes of therapy for depression is music therapy. Creating a playlist of positive songs and listening to it can raise our spirits. Nowadays most of us have devices set up in our homes that, with a simple verbal request, can share with us words of hope. These melodies remind us of moments when we sensed God's presence during times of worship. People battling depression often describe it as spiritual darkness. If we can identify what we are feeling and where we are feeling it, we can then use the movements of singing, dancing, or raising our hands to allow our bodies to experience an emotional and spiritual release.

So, what is the difference between the depressive mindset and depression? The depressive mindset occurs when negative thinking begins to invade a person's thought life. With clinical depression, negative thinking usually exists along with body chemistry changes impacting behaviors, like sleeping, eating, energy level, and motivation.

When we have a depressive mindset, we may still have trouble with these behaviors, but they are transitional, lasting only a few days to a few weeks and are often triggered by negative circumstances. However, clinical depression—including dysthymia, a mild, low-grade depression—intensifies the symptoms to a different level. With clinical depression negativity is more frequent, and the feelings of sadness, apathy, irritability, and lack of energy are far more extreme. When depression becomes severe, it prevents you from experiencing joy and freedom and from living out your life purposes. Severe depression may even tempt you to consider whether you want to keep living. Resist this idea and get help immediately.

If you are struggling with severe depression, you need to consult a trained professional with no shame for seeking help. So many women breathe a sigh of relief when they share with me about their depressive symptoms for the first time. They realize they are not alone and there are solutions. And almost all of them remark they wish they had sought help sooner.

Mindset Movement 1: *Fold a paper in half and complete the exercise described above. Write out your new God-based statements or a Scripture that combats your negative thought(s) on sticky notes and display them where you can rehearse them. Set an alarm on your phone to remind you to retrain your brain.*

Mindset Movement 2: *The next time you feel stuck in a negative emotion, move your body. Go for a walk, get up from your desk and go to the bathroom, or stretch and take a deep breath.*

Mindset Movement 3: *If you feel you need a mental health checkup, make an appointment with a trusted doctor, see if your church has a referral list, or look for a Christian counselor in your area. Don't let living in a small town deter you. With telehealth you can find well-equipped counselors who can treat you throughout your state.*

Chapter Five

The Discontented Mindset—Battling Comparison and Pride

"Don't love money; be satisfied with what you have. For God has said, 'I will never fail you. I will never abandon you.'"

—Hebrews 13:5, NLT

"I don't want it!"

My toddler had the biggest look of disgust on his face as I tried to feed him the split pea soup. He was not going to budge on his position either. Oh, the battles mamas go through just trying to make their tribe happy. Feeding our families or otherwise providing for them is often a thankless job. But this time I was prepared to go to the mat. I was going to do battle, and I was going to win.

I Can't Get No Satisfaction

As my child closed his lips and shook his head, the battle lines were drawn. I offered the same soup to him meal after meal, but his mindset was fixed. So was mine. This is a picture of our mindsets. Once we make up our mind, it is hard to let go of our perspective.

But fixed mindsets can become growth mindsets. At the fourth meal of split pea soup, my son was getting a little tired of this charade. He gave in. Suddenly, the once firmly shut mouth opened wide, ready to receive the spoon airplane. And it happened. He smiled a great big smile.

"This is my favorite soup now!" he said.

"Oh, thank God," I thought. "Thank God!"

My son was satisfied because he chose to accept what was being offered. He could have been satisfied earlier, but he would not allow it. Then he made up his mind to think differently, to take a risk. It paid off. Sometimes we must let go of our ideas in order to be satisfied.

If our discontented attitude can be fixed while we are young, it would spare us a lot of pain when we are older. The main game in our culture is pursuing the American dream. So many of us spend our lives chasing after material success and security, thinking when we have amassed enough goods and money, then we will be happy. But having our contentment based on fallen culture is setting ourselves up for failure.

Our souls are not made for things. Statuses and positions cannot satisfy us either—at least not for the long haul. Then, when we put pressure on our relationships to deliver relief for the craving of our souls, our relationships oftentimes can't withstand that pressure and break down. No one and nothing can fill the space God is meant to occupy. So, while we try to find contentment through things or positions or human relationships, God has so much better for us.

The Grass Isn't Greener

If my son's siblings were munching on a dessert while he was offered split pea soup, he would not have ever tried the green stuff his mama was feeding him. And he would have missed out. Comparison can rob us of contentment. Our minds get stuck saying what we have isn't enough or what someone else has is what we need. Somehow what others have must be better. But someone else's portion cannot satisfy us. God intends something very specific for each of His children.

Comparison began in the Garden of Eden when Cain wanted what Abel had—only it wasn't something material he wanted. Cain was jealous for the praise his brother received. Abel's offering pleased God, but Cain's didn't. The shame from that moment ignited anger and hatred.

Our flesh wants to be prized above others. But a quest to be best won't be blessed. Ultimately, this is self-worship. Ironically, this won't satisfy us either. Because worshiping something less (ourselves) than the best (God) just creates more of a relentless hunger. We were made to worship One who is higher than us. The psalmist said it well in Psalm 61:2, "... Lead me to the rock that is higher than I" (ESV). We become discontented when we compare our lot to what seems better in our eyes.

Being Ruled by Our Wants

Discontentment is an entitled state of mind that believes we deserve better. When my youngest son was little, he had a habit of randomly taking things that weren't his. If he wanted it, he took it. End of story. Time and again I would tell him that taking things would never satisfy him.

If we don't rule our wants, our wants will rule us. My son was not content with what he had, and his eyes always wanted what someone else had. While we easily see this behavior in our children, sometimes we adults also need a reminder that God satisfies us with good things. God's provision might not always be what we want, but it is what we need. "For he satisfies the longing soul, and the hungry soul he fills with good things" (Psalm 107:9, ESV).

Will we let God satisfy us? Or will we seek to satisfy ourselves? When we adopted our youngest son from Russia, he did not want to eat anything other than what he knew: porridge. (One son hated split pea soup, and the other loved porridge. Go figure.) We wanted to give him better food, but he was not interested. We even took him to a nice restaurant and bought him a favorite kid's meal—French fries, hamburger, soda. He would have none of it.

Then, the next morning was a different story. Ten pancakes and 20 ounces of juice later, a smile formed on his face. Satisfaction. His wants had been programmed for what had been provided, for lesser things. Sometimes we stay fixed on our wants because we don't see what God has for us. And sometimes we are led by our wants because we have an orphan mindset. We want what others have, but our loving Father who adopted us wants the best for each one of us.

Keep Your Eye on the Prize

The flesh is never satisfied. This is a problem. Our wants can drive us to discontentment as we strive for things outside of God's will. Solomon likened the wants of the flesh to hell. "Just as death and destruction are never satisfied, so human desire is never satisfied" (Proverbs 27:20, NLT). This is strong imagery. What we want could lead us far away from God if our wants are not according to His will and plan. What we fix our eyes on can either ignite lust or curb dissatisfaction. We need to train our eyes and minds to want what God wants for us.

Money, Money, Money

We are programmed by the media and our surrounding culture to chase after the next latest, greatest thing. But materialism and money can be a trap if our heart is set on them. "For the love of money is a root of all kinds of evil. Some people, eager for money, have wandered from the faith and pierced themselves with many griefs" (1 Timothy 6:10, NIV). God knows what we need. Craving beyond His provision will never satisfy us. Everything we own will eventually rot, so hoping in things that fade will always leave us wanting.

This is the cause of the discontented mindset. We need to set our mind on things that satisfy. We need to deprogram our mindset from the worldly focus of wants and reprogram it to God's desire for us and His world. We house the Holy Spirit. Craving earthly things will only leave us hungry. But craving spiritual things will cause us to seek what will fill our souls to overflowing.

Being satisfied with what God provides is worship. Such contentment expresses a relationship with God that trusts He is always enough. "Don't love money; be satisfied with what you have. For God has said, 'I will never fail you. I will never abandon you'" (Hebrews 13:5, NLT). God is with us. We have our greatest need fulfilled if we recognize it. However, at times our wants, likes, or dislikes have nothing to do with greed. Sometimes discontentment arises simply because we do not get our way.

A Lesson from Jonah

"The word of the LORD came to Jonah the son of Amittai, saying, 'Arise, go to Nineveh, the great city, and cry out against it, because their wickedness has come up before Me.' But Jonah got up to flee to Tarshish from the presence of the LORD" (Jonah 1:1-3a, NASB). God had a plan for Jonah and sent him on a mission. But Jonah was not happy with God's plans or provision. So Jonah ran away from God and His plans.

The thing is, we can't run away from our problems or our discontented mindset. Trying to outrun the presence of God is, well, impossible. Jonah tried to sail away from his problems, but those problems came along for the ride as well. Not only did Jonah's disobedience to God and his discontentment with God's plans affect him, they also almost cost the lives of those around him.

As the sea became tumultuous due to Jonah's sinful mindset, the ship's crew looked among them to see if anyone had caused this anger from God. "So the captain came and said to him, 'What do you mean, you sleeper? Arise, call out to your god! Perhaps the god will give a thought to us, that we may not perish' (Jonah 1:6, ESV).

Then the men cast lots to determine who was to blame and the lot fell to Jonah. When they asked him what he had done, Jonah admitted it: "And he said to them, 'I am a Hebrew, and I fear the LORD, the God of heaven, who made the sea and the dry land.' Then the men were exceedingly afraid and said to him, 'What is this that you have done!' For the men knew that he was fleeing from the presence of the LORD, because he had told them" (Jonah 1:9-10, ESV). For someone who feared God, Jonah was not acting like it.

When we are discontent, we can't be sent. Although it may be easy to judge Jonah for his obvious disobedience, perhaps we can also recognize discontentment in our own life when we find ourselves in circumstances we do not desire. Jonah's discontent stemmed from comparison and jealousy. Nineveh was essentially sin city. The citizens there were enemies of God's people. Jonah could not understand why God desired to spare those evil people.

Sometimes we let our reason trump God's will. We think we know better. Ultimately, Jonah did not want God's will. While I cannot fathom running away from God, much like Jonah, I have wondered why God allows certain people to get away with heinous sin. In the past I have struggled to trust God and have kept Him at a distance after the "Ninevites" in my own life caused ruin and wreckage.

Running away from God isn't only a physical action; it can happen in our souls as well. Though our souls are prone to wander, God loves us too much to leave us where we don't understand His will. God pursued Jonah to the bottom of the sea. Yep, His presence was there, too. And there in the middle of the sea, Jonah cried out to God:

> "While I was fainting away, I remembered the LORD, and my prayer came to You, into Your holy temple. Those who are followers of worthless idols abandon their faithfulness, but I will sacrifice to You with a voice of thanksgiving. That which I

have vowed I will pay. Salvation is from the Lord" (Jonah 2:7-9, NASB).

Did you catch what turned around Jonah's discontentment? He remembered God. Jonah remembered God's faithfulness and snapped out of his stubborn mindset that had been fixed on his own way. Jonah laid down his idols and picked up gratitude. When we feel discontented, counting our blessings is not just a nice thing to do; it might save our life.

My Way or the Highway

Jonah's desire to do things his way led him far away from God's plan and landed him in the belly of a big fish. God is patient. He is willing to teach us lessons the hard way, but it would be far better just to trust Him and do things His way. Clinging to our own plans is dangerous considering whose will is ultimately going to be done. "Many are the plans in the mind of a man, but it is the purpose of the Lord that will stand" (Proverbs 19:21, ESV).

When we cling to our own ways rather than God's, we are clinging to idols. These idols will eventually cause us discontentment with God's plans. However, when we live under the Lordship of Jesus Christ, we stop resisting His plans realizing they are best. "The heart of man plans his way, but the Lord establishes his steps" (Proverbs 16:9, ESV).

When we lay down what we think we deserve and pick up only what is God's will for us, surprisingly we can be content with not getting what we want. Most things cannot satisfy us anyway. Recognizing the triggers of discontentment can teach us to want God's way and not our own. In the end, God's will won't be thwarted. Besides, if we could see what God sees, we wouldn't want it any other way.

Trigger 1: Comparison

Discontentment is often shaped by jealousy, which begins with comparison as we try to measure up to others around us. I remember such a time in my life. Oh, how I wanted to be like the others when I was in middle school. I convinced myself that the acceptance of a certain group of ballplayers was all that mattered.

At the first practice I wanted to show my classmates I was tough like them; all 4 feet 11 inches of me. I had the "tough girl" squint down as I walked into the batter's box. My hands choked up the bat as I crouched in the most intimidating stance I could offer. I was going to slam that ball to kingdom come.

Baseball was in my blood, so to speak. One of my older brothers had aspirations of playing in the major leagues, and I had spent many afternoons pitching a tape ball to him (not a real baseball, mind you, to keep from getting hurt). I desperately wanted to be an athlete like my brothers, to be accepted among the athletes. My only problem was I was no athlete.

Sure, I could hit the ball, but man, did I run slow. And when it came time to catch the ball in the outfield, the sun made it difficult for my sensitive eyes to see straight. I tried my best at whatever activity came up, but I never quite felt like I belonged. When my classmates moved on to the next thing, I worked hard to excel at that, too, so I could gain their acceptance. However, when I finally found my area of aptitude—the euphonium!—it was not so esteemed by others.

I never found that fulfilling sense of belonging in middle school. I needed to learn real belonging was not based on merit, talent, or popularity—all uncertain things. Comparison to others will only leave us discontented. As we recognize that we never measure up, we can find our contentment in Christ's acceptance.

We are wired to want to belong. This can lead to comparison and competitive behavior, stemming from the desire to be connected and accepted in our relentless hunt for identity. But we discover that there is a two-edged sword to belonging in any group. Fitting in isn't the same as belonging. We will never perfectly fit anywhere on this earth. Our citizenship is in Heaven. Comparing ourselves to others cheapens our true identity, and it is never satisfied.

Trigger 2: Pride

The discontented mindset is also steeped in pride and an inordinate amount of thinking of how to please self. We just don't understand why people don't think like we do or want to do things our way. The foolish statement from one of Frank Sinatra's songs echoes the heart of man, "I Did It My Way." Truly, God is the One who enables us to do anything. There's no room for pride there. When we see our need of God's perspective and humbly renew our mind to His way, we can let go of pride. But it will be a constant process.

King Nebuchadnezzar's pride cost him his crown and caused him to crawl around like an animal. He had everything the world could offer but gave himself the glory for it—until he came to his right mindset. "After this time had passed, I, Nebuchadnezzar, looked up to heaven. My sanity returned, and I praised and worshiped the Most High and honored the one who lives forever …" (Daniel 4:34a, NLT).

The prideful mind is set on our own glory. We don't think rightly when self is on the throne. Christ alone is the one holy, perfect One. Thinking on the one Higher One gives us a right mind. When we acknowledge and glorify God—what we are created to do—we restore our mind. If Christ who was God in the flesh took a humble position, how much more should we?

> "Have this mind among yourselves, which is yours in Christ Jesus, who, though he was in the form of God, did not count equality with God a thing to be grasped, but emptied himself, by taking the form of a servant, being born in the likeness of men. And being found in human form, he humbled himself by becoming obedient to the point of death, even death on a cross" (Philippians 2:5-8, ESV).

We can have the mind of Christ and already do (1 Corinthians 2:16). Christ had a servant's heart. Christ did not think of Himself. Christ came in our identity so He could give us His. Christ humbled Himself in obedience. When we are tempted to think we deserve more, we can think on Christ who definitely deserved more but left it all to win our souls. When we think it is impossible to adopt the mind of Christ, we can also realize that God's Word tells us to have this mind. God would not tell us to if we couldn't.

Trigger 3: Ingratitude

Ingratitude is another ugly root to our discontentment. It comes from an entitled attitude that wants more, not recognizing how blessed we already are. God's inheritance for us is so much greater than anything on this earth. Our souls will not be satisfied with temporary things. "Set your minds on things that are above, not on things that are on earth" (Colossians 3:2 ESV).

On the final eve before Christ's crucifixion, the Bible says Jesus, at 33 years of age, knew His time was near. By our world's standard that seems unfair. He should have had a wife and a long life, lots of belongings, children. And He should not have to suffer, let alone die, for someone else's sin. But Christ submitted to the Father's will. If He had gone outside of that will, no one would be saved.

If God used Christ's suffering for good, how could God use our unfortunate circumstances? When we are dissatisfied with God's provision, we need to have Christ's vision. People want to seize all the pleasure from this life they can. As counterintuitive as it seems, it is denying our flesh its desired pleasure that produces true contentment.

When I was a child, I remember being asked what I would do if I knew I had only five minutes to live. Most of my peers said they would go and commit that sin they'd been wanting to do. (Y'all, I went to a secular school.) Most of my current friends would probably say they would spend their last five minutes telling their close friends and family how much they love them. In Jesus' final moments, He chose to wash His disciples' feet. The Bible says Jesus loved His spiritual children to the end (John 13:1). I don't know about you, but if I knew I was about to be murdered, washing other people's feet would not be on my list of priorities. But Christ was not discontent with His circumstances. He was living into them in the will of God.

Trigger 4: Unbelief

The enemy attacks our belief system, provoking us to doubt the goodness of God and to set our minds on our own plan. When we choose to go against God's will, we are believing a lie, or a whole pack of lies. When we go our own way, we are thinking the following: God isn't enough. God's way isn't good. We must figure out our own way.

All these false beliefs form a narrative that is like Jonah's. We must counter our unbelief by adopting a different mindset and choosing to believe Christ over all else. In the Gospel of John, Christ was telling His disciples to believe in His good plans for them. "Do not let your heart be troubled; believe in God, believe also in Me. In My Father's house are many rooms; if that were not so, I would have told you, because I am going there to prepare a place for you" (John 14:1-2, NASB).

The Greek word for "heart" is *kardia*. It is synonymous with the soul or mind and is defined as the "seat of the thoughts, passions, desires, appetites, affections, purposes, endeavors, having to do with our understanding, our intelligence, will or character."[15] Christ was appealing to the mind of the disciples. They could make up their mind not to give in to fear. The word for "believe" is the Greek word *pisteúō*, and it means literally "to think to be true."[16] We all believe lies and need to retrain our brains. The world system affects our thoughts. Without realizing it, we can subscribe to worldviews that don't center around God and believe that things in this world can satisfy us.

We can easily forget Jesus is enough. Do we truly believe He is? Or is it only a religious saying? A Christian culture is not the same as a fervent faith that trusts God and His Word. Jesus repeatedly told us that what He said is true. Sometimes it will take repetition to crack through our false belief systems that inhibit true contentment.

Trigger 5: Idolatry

God said to have no idols. However, our idols are not always so obvious. Wanting our way can become idolatry, especially when we cannot be content with a plan that is not our own. Mind renewal helps us to reorient ourselves to worshiping God rather than our way. Paul understood the battle of the mind and challenged us to choose transformation: "Do not be conformed to this world, but be transformed by the renewal of your mind, that by testing you may discern what is the will of God, what is good and acceptable and perfect" (Romans 12:2, ESV).

We have been conformed to a pattern we did not create and neither did God. But we can be transformed as we renew our mind with truth and toward God's will, not ours. It will no doubt take effort to undo our stubborn flesh that urges us toward our own wants. But when we sense the discontent mindset rising, that is a warning sign. We don't have to keep behaving in the same way when we dutifully obeyed our discontentment. We can examine our thoughts to see if they are of God or of the world.

The lust of the flesh, lust of the eyes, and boastful pride of life are not of God. As the apostle John shared, "For the world offers only a craving for physical pleasure, a craving for everything we see, and pride in our achievements and possessions. These are not from the Father, but are from this world" (1 John 2:16, NLT). It will be hard at first to lay down what we were trying so hard to gain. But the truth is, we would never attain the end to our desire anyway because the eyes are never satisfied. But when our minds are renewed with God's will, we understand what is good and acceptable and perfect, and we learn we can tell our flesh "no".

The Power of Humility

God hates the proud. That's a pretty good motivation to seek humility, right? But this world does not esteem the humble. Most people's mode of operation is to be self-made. But there is incredible power within the truly humble. They are not bent on getting their way and are freed from the burden of self. We find peace when we let go of what we never controlled in the first place. Truly only Christ was the perfect humble person, but below are some tips that can help form a humble heart and content mindset.

Tip 1: Gratitude

Since ingratitude contributes to our discontentment, its opposite, gratitude, helps produce contentment. It is not enough to say, "Don't be ungrateful." Putting on gratitude by intentionally thanking God and others for things we take for granted helps to cultivate a right heart. When we do this, complaining gets kicked to the curb.

"... Put on the new self, which is being renewed in knowledge after the image of its creator. ... Put on then, as God's chosen ones, holy and beloved, compassionate hearts, kindness, humility, meekness, and patience" (Colossians 3:10, 12, ESV). We cannot "put on" if we have not first "put off." We must first put off ingratitude by asking God to open our eyes to what we have taken for granted. We don't own our blessings. When they are taken away, we can still choose to be grateful by the grace of God. True gratitude springs up when there doesn't seem to be much to be grateful for.

Tip 2: Trust

Paired with the trigger of unbelief, trust is a tricky antidote. Trust requires faith when we cannot see an answer. But trust does not require blind faith. To put trust into action, first we must tear down any faulty trust we had. Trusting in things that are not promised leads to discontent. This happens when our mindsets are corrupted by this world. That's when we need to shift our mindset to look at and trust in God, not self or outcomes. This trust is not half-hearted and not reliant on self at all.

"The LORD is my strength and shield. I trust him with all my heart. He helps me, and my heart is filled with joy. I burst out in songs of thanksgiving." (Psalm 28:7, NLT). The Hebrew word for *heart* in this verse comes from the word *lêb,*[17] which in the Septuagint, the Greek Old Testament translation, is the same Greek word *kardia,* the place where we make up our mind. God wants our whole heart and mind. Our hearts chase after so many things we place our trust in. But only One deserves our trust and can fulfill it. God is trustworthy.

Tip 3: Obedience

When we give in to negative mindsets, we are choosing to believe and obey the lies and thoughts that flow in and out of our minds rather than believing and obeying Jesus. Negative mindsets enslave us to obey the principles of this world. Paul warned the church at Galatia not to go backward into its former way of thinking.

> "Formerly, when you did not know God, you were enslaved to those that by nature are not gods. But now that you have come to know God, or rather to be known by God, how can you turn back again to the weak and worthless elementary principles of the world, whose slaves you want to be once more?" (Galatians 4:8-9, ESV).

When we recognize a mindset can enslave us to disobedience, we see our need to be free from negative mindsets. We don't have to stay stuck when Christ is our sufficiency. Mindsets cannot deliver what our souls desire. Obeying God instead of our mindsets helps to set us free from obedience to lesser things that could dominate our thoughts and life. In the end, we are commanded to obey God.

Tip 4: Be Holy

The command to be holy has our best interest at heart. Rather than pursuing personal gain, which is where our mindsets can get stuck, we are set free when we pursue holiness. Holiness requires that we prepare our minds. We need to evaluate what we think about. It is not holy to be discontented or to be prideful. Peter encouraged the Church to set its mind on holiness rather than worldliness.

> "Therefore, preparing your minds for action, and being sober-minded, set your hope fully on the grace that will be brought to you at the revelation of Jesus Christ. As obedient children, do not be conformed to the passions of your former igno-

> rance, but as he who called you is holy, you also be holy in all your conduct" (1 Peter 1:13-15, ESV).

Tip 5: Die to Self

A college professor during my undergraduate years once remarked that teaching me was like trying to train a wild horse. But he said it was better than trying to teach a wooden one. We need to be fully alive, passionately living for Jesus. Yet we also need to die to self. This sounds like a paradox, but the truth is we really live when we die to self.

How can this be? Our mindsets are naturally bent toward self. When we gear them toward others and toward God's glory, that is when we live worthy lives no longer wasted on selfish pursuits. Paul had a lot to say about dying to self and being freed from the enslavement of the flesh: "But thanks be to God, that you who were once slaves of sin have become obedient from the heart to the standard of teaching to which you were committed, and, having been set free from sin, have become slaves of righteousness" (Romans 6:17-18, ESV).

Where does this obedience come from? The mind/heart. There's that word again: *kardia*. Our heart, or mind, is where the magic happens. We must choose to make up our mind to die to our way of thinking to find the freedom to rise above negative mindsets and be righteous.

Getting to the Root

Comparison is the thief of joy. This statement, attributed to President Theodore Roosevelt, reveals what a discontented mindset does to us. It steals our joy. Frankly, all the negative mindsets are thieves in their own way. Discontentment sprouts from jealousy, pride, and comparison. It's a miserable taskmaster. But when we understand our mind has become focused on worldly hopes, we can choose to cultivate a kingdom mentality that cheers for everyone else rather than our own gain. Instead of withholding from others—which never satisfies our jealous hearts—we can develop a generous mindset and gain contentment by putting others first.

Mindset of Christ

Not even Christ sought His own will. "For even Christ did not please Himself" (Romans 15:3a, NIV). "He was oppressed, and he was afflicted, yet he opened not his mouth; like a lamb that is led to the slaughter, and like a sheep that before its shearers is silent, so he opened not his mouth" (Isaiah 53:7, ESV). Jesus came to serve rather than to be served. He did not pursue His own contentment. Jesus showed us how to be content by not living according to the pattern of this world. And He said we aren't of this world either: "They are not of the world, just as I am not of the world" (John 17:16, ESV).

Mind Renewal: Keys to Unlock Our Mind

Key Thought:

We are not discontent any longer when we renew our mind to crave the things of Heaven instead of the things of earth.

Key Verse: Truth from God's Word

"Set your minds on things that are above, not on things that are on earth" (Colossians 3:2, ESV).

Key Change: Application—Replacing Comparison and Finding Contentment

Paul reminded us about the secret to finding contentment. "I know how to live on almost nothing or with everything. I have learned the secret of living in every situation, whether it is with a full stomach or empty, with plenty or little. For I can do everything through Christ, who gives me strength" (Philippians 4:12-13, NLT).

Right now, pray and ask God to reveal discontentment in your life, and ask Christ for strength to be content in that thing. There are no limits on this. Paul said he was content with everything. We can be that way, too.

Counselor's Corner

I often use the phrase "stay in your own lane" during therapy. In our culture, we can easily become distracted—and subsequently jealous or prideful—by constantly looking at others' lives. This practice often begins during childhood.

When we were children, we tended to compare what our siblings got to what we got. So what's the problem with wanting to be someone else or have what they have? The habit of constant comparison robs us of living out our own purposes for being on this earth. As we focus on our own strengths, gifts, and calling, we concentrate our energy in developing into the people God created us to be, to impact our world like each of us was designed to do. When we fix our eyes on our God-given prize, we will run our specific race and not someone else's. When we stop comparing our life to others' lives, we will experience a higher level of contentment.

How can we begin this process? One great way is getting to know ourselves and why we were created. I often assign my clients homework so they can learn more about what they value, what their strengths and abilities are, and how they approach life. Learning our top strengths in Strengthfinders and our God-given spiritual gifts can help us discover what we're good at and understand what motivates us. Using personality assessments can empower us to know ourselves and gain confidence in working toward fulfilling our destiny.

Our purposes occur in seasons, and these change throughout our lives. Some of us are currently stay-at-home moms, nurturing our preschool children. Some of us are empty nesters, figuring out life after our children have established their independence. Some of us are career women, developing our abilities, serving others, and impacting our world in a variety of professions. We can all benefit by taking time to define our purpose according to the season we are in.

When we interact with our kids at home, who do we want to be and what do we want to model? How about at work with our coworkers? Knowing how we are designed and what we are called to do in each season of our lives gives us confidence to thrive in our daily lives.

When we focus on knowing ourselves and joining with God to be the women He created us to be, we don't have the time or energy to compare ourselves to others. When we catch ourselves doing so, we can apply the following three actions. These practices will not only protect us from letting comparison overwhelm us, but they will also create positive emotions in our body when we notice someone else's success.

- We can celebrate people's successes. Being excited for others feels much better than feeling sorry for ourselves.
- We can let others' successes inspire us to learn something new. If this new interest becomes important to us, we can look for a course, mentor or support group to help us develop in that area.
- We can remember that ultimately God is the source. When we remind ourselves we are the vessels or messengers, and all of us are working together for the same goal, we can be excited to see God on the move—in our lives and the lives of others.

Mindset Movement: *Create a phrase like "stay in your lane" to use when you are tempted to compare.*

Chapter Six

The Doubtful Mindset—Battling Unbelief and Hopelessness

"*I would have lost heart,* unless I had believed That I would see the goodness of the LORD In the land of the living. Wait on the LORD; Be of good courage, And He shall strengthen your heart; Wait, I say, on the LORD!

—Psalm 27:13-14, NKJV

We all know people who are "Debbie Downers," or shall I say, "Debbie Doubters." Like Doubting Thomas, the apostle, they won't believe it unless they see it. They are skeptical, realists who are maybe even a tad jaded.

There is good in this temperament though. Such people are not gullible, for sure. But they can miss out on the upside and potential of every challenging situation if they don't choose faith where doubt looms large. They might build walls that keep them safe as they let doubt protect them from the pain of the "what if's," but those walls also keep out faith and real hope.

What Does God's Goodness Mean?

David faced many fears during his life. Doubts could have easily won out. But he did not give in to his doubt even as real enemies taunted him to do so. David was raw and real about the doubts filling his mind, and he chose to wait on God rather than to give in to fear.

David wrote the above verses from Psalm 27 when he was once again encountering enemies. These words have become a refuge for me during difficult experiences. At the time when I first studied these verses, I thought God's goodness meant the removal of my problems. But when the problems remained, it was contemplating God's goodness that gave me comfort.

Could I still trust in God? Was there a promise in these verses, or was I misinterpreting them? As I worshiped God and cried out to Him, I realized I could see God's goodness right in the midst of severe pain. I did not have to be on the other side of the problem to be able to see God's goodness, and it was His goodness that got me through the pain. Doubting God would not have helped me but focusing on how God is greater than my problems would.

Whether we are glass half full or half empty people, we all will battle the doubtful mindset at some point. Usually, some kind of pain initiates this struggle. Like the psalmist who proclaimed the goodness of the Lord right in the middle of the "badness" of life, we, too, will see what our faith is made of when we encounter pain, whether it is physical, mental, or spiritual. Will we choose to believe and hope, or will we give in to the doubt? Our mindset will be a determining factor.

When Less Becomes More

Doubting offers us no comfort. It is a protective measure we use to prevent us from being duped or hurt by something untrustworthy, but it is a false comfort. The lens of the doubtful mindset keeps us trapped in a "less" mentality. When we act on unbelief and doubt, we will reap its consequences. However, when we take a risk and act on faith, we will reap beautiful fruit in so doing.

Doubts are lies whispered to our souls, but they are laced with enough truth to help us swallow them whole. When we do, we become paralyzed, unable to choose true hope. We have the power to overcome our doubt through Christ when we replace our "less" mentalities with the "more" fullness found in God's truth.

Exposing the lie behind common doubts, we can choose to replace former doubts with God's Word and promises, which never fail. Doubt can keep us stuck. We dare not hope for more. But hope has a way of prying us free from doubt's snare. The following are some of the "less" feelings that doubting brings:

- **Powerless, defined by our weakness:** We don't have enough willpower. We cannot choose to do or even to think about what we should do or think. Can you say pink elephants?
- **Useless, defined by our ability:** We can't do anything right. We are not good enough.
- **Helpless, defined by our willpower:** There is no help that will really last. We're not strong enough.
- **Meaningless, defined by our view:** Nothing really matters. This life or what we have is not enough.

- **Worthless, defined by our value**: Our value is based on works. We are not enough.
- **Hopeless, defined by our prospects:** There is no ultimate good outcome, or the foundational grace of God is not enough.

Thinking negatively does things to our mind, making us bitter, angry, sad, and doubtful—all mindsets centered on self. These thoughts are ungodly, or not Godlike, and are unhealthy for us. God invites us to think like Him.

The doubtful definitions above all describe the person. They become a part of our identity. Also, they all emphasize the word "enough." Doubters never have enough. The irony is we discover we have enough when we admit we don't. In another words, when we acknowledge our lack and accept our need of God, that's when we are assured.

Judging ourselves by our own plumb line is a surefire path to uncertainty. When we look at life through a doubtful mindset, life will always appear dismal. But when our identity is in Christ, His strength and capabilities, less becomes more. When we notice our doubtful mindset, thinking there's no way we can change, we can take a risky step and ask God to help us believe we can. How do we escape the "Less Land" that doubtful mindsets bring? By traveling on higher ground.

Taking the High Road

A prescription for a right mind is found in Philippians 4:8. We likely know this verse by heart, but let's read it again like the first time: "Finally, brothers and sisters, whatever is true, whatever is noble, whatever is right, whatever is pure, whatever is lovely, whatever is admirable—if anything is excellent or praiseworthy—think about such things" (Philippians 4:8, NIV).

As we begin to see God's perspective and adopt His mindset, we are set free to live on higher ground. No longer encumbered by the demands of a carnal mindset, we are free to choose differently, and peace and hope are born. This is power, indeed.

- **Whatever is true: We are not powerless.** We must not entertain lies. Doubts are lies. We can examine our thoughts through the lens of Scripture. God alone is the source of truth (Romans 3:4). We can do all things through Christ (Philippians 4:13).
- **Whatever is noble: We are not useless in Christ.** We must not let shame take away the honor we have in Christ. Instead, we can reflect on the identity we have been given. The old is gone; the new has come (2 Corinthians 5:17). We can cultivate righteous thinking and think of God's possibilities, which are always higher than our own.
- **Whatever is right: We are not helpless.** When everything around us is wrong, Christ is our true north. We are in the world and can think like the world easily enough. The Greek word for "right" is *dikaios,* and it means to act in conformity with the will of God. Thinking biblically overcomes doubts that thinking according to the world's standards causes.
- **Whatever is pure: Life is not meaningless.** We are called to be holy and to live for God. There is no higher honor. Being holy in an unholy world is not normal or easy. But it is joyful and possible. Maintaining purity starts in our thought life and results in our actions. We are to be holy as God is holy (1 Peter 1:15).

- **Whatever is lovely: We are not worthless in Christ.** Friends, we are beautiful creations made by a God who loves us. That is the truth. Our appearance never was supposed to determine our worth. Our worth cannot be described. Recognizing what is beautiful will require changing the lens we view through. When we understand what true beauty is, we rise above the superficial concepts of beauty in the world.
- **Whatever is excellent: We are not hopeless because Christ gave His very best.** Christ deserves our very best, too. When our thinking is excellent, we rise above the hope dashers of our day. Thinking on lesser things will not get us to higher ground. We can train our brain to think rightly. What a hope this is!

Mr. Positivity

Some of us cannot stand super positive people, and we know we will never be like them. That's OK. The goal to overcoming a doubtful mindset is not simply positivity, unicorns, and roses. It is a rewiring of how we think. Apostle Paul was not exhorting the Church into positive thinking. He was encouraging fellow believers to allow Christ to change their whole mindsets. Rather than allowing ourselves to be jaded by realism, we can let our faith guide our choices and reflect upon what God tells us instead of doubt.

Before Paul wrote what the Church should think about in Philippians 4:8, he told the church in Philippi what *not* to think about to gain peace: "Do not be anxious about anything, but in everything by prayer and supplication with thanksgiving let your requests be made known to God. And the peace of God, which surpasses all understanding, will guard your hearts and your minds in Christ Jesus" (Philippians 4:6-7 ESV).

Doubting produces anxiety. It leaves us fearful of outcomes rather than peaceful no matter what the outcome is. We access a *faith*-ful mindset through prayer and being honest about our needs—this is what supplication is. Being ambivalent is not faith. It does not bring security. God will give us peace when we are willing to risk believing Him rather than our doubts.

Finding Faith in God in Hard Places

Doubting is part of the battlefield we face as we seek to apply the mind of Christ in a fallen world. Life is hard. How we interpret the hard places can impact our faith and how we live. Peter can teach us a few things about doubt. He surely had his moments of failure in that area, but he took risks and did not stay bound in uncertainty. Consequently, he grew from his risks and became the rock on which Christ built His Church. Doubting did not preclude Peter from being used by God in mighty ways.

Lessons from Peter

We smile when we think of Peter. Big waves tossing a boat to and fro are enough to make any of us whimper and cling for dear life. But Peter asked Jesus to help him walk on those waves:

> "But when the disciples saw him walking on the sea, they were terrified, and said, 'It is a ghost!' and they cried out in fear. But immediately Jesus spoke to them, saying, 'Take heart; it is I. Do not

> be afraid.' And Peter answered him, 'Lord, if it is you, command me to come to you on the water.' He said, 'Come.' So Peter got out of the boat and walked on the water and came to Jesus. But when he saw the wind, he was afraid, and beginning to sink he cried out, 'Lord, save me.' Jesus immediately reached out his hand and took hold of him, saying to him, 'O you of little faith, why did you doubt?'" (Matthew 14:26-31, ESV).

Waves of doubt easily arise in our lives. When they come, we want to run, duck, and hide, unless we think like Jesus and Peter in the moment above. What keeps us from walking on the waves of doubt instead of being submerged by them?

Trigger 1: Fear of Harm

Fear was behind the doubt that provoked Peter, causing him to take his eyes off Jesus and focus on his circumstances. Peter knew Christ had authority to command, but his mindset shifted. In a nanosecond Peter chose to not believe Jesus' command but to believe the fear and doubt in his head instead. We cannot have both faith and doubt together. One must win out. Which will it be? We must make up our mind to trust God's Word. God said it. I believe it. That settles it.

When we recite Scripture repeatedly, it will convince our flesh. God is able, friends! If even the disciples struggled with doubt from time to time, we will, too. But we can walk on those waves together. The perfect love of God casts out all fear. Fearing harm more than God means we doubt His ability to protect us, which He promised to do. And God never breaks His promises.

Trigger 2: Closed-Minded Attitude

Doubt does not just arise from fear of physical circumstances. It can also rise in our souls when we doubt the will of God. This negative mindset equates to being closed-minded; we are not open to a plan we can't wrap our mind around.

Peter doubted Jesus' plan. It did not make sense to him. Jesus was God in the flesh and Peter's hero. As such, He was supposed to save them; not suffer, and die.

> "From that time Jesus began to show his disciples that he must go to Jerusalem and suffer many things from the elders and chief priests and scribes, and be killed, and on the third day be raised. And Peter took him aside and began to rebuke him, saying, 'Far be it from you, Lord! This shall never happen to you.' But he turned and said to Peter, 'Get behind me, Satan! You are a hindrance to me. For you are not setting your mind on the things of God, but on the things of man'" (Matthew 16:21-23, ESV).

Jesus told Peter that he was setting his mind on the things of man. Fixed mindsets can disable us from seeing any other point of view. Certainly, we need to block out worldly mindsets, but we also need minds open to transformation from the Word of God.

Trigger 3: Fear of Man

Peter learned a lot about trusting Jesus, but even he made mistakes. Peter said he would go with Jesus to the end, but the fear of man shut that faithful mindset down. Peer pressure can take our mindset and cause us to compromise our beliefs. Peter allowed doubt to creep in because of what others thought, which led him to do the unthinkable: deny Jesus.

> "Then Jesus said to them, 'You will all fall away because of me this night. For it is written, "I will strike the shepherd, and the sheep of the flock will be scattered." But after I am raised up, I will go before you to Galilee.' Peter answered him, 'Though they all fall away because of you, I will never fall away.' Jesus said to him, 'Truly, I tell you, this very night, before the rooster crows, you will deny me three times.' Peter said to him, 'Even if I must die with you, I will not deny you!' And all the disciples said the same" (Matthew 26:31-35, ESV).

God already knows we are going to fail. He knows our mindsets vacillate. Jesus even prepared Peter for this difficult test of loyalty, yet Peter quickly swatted three strikes. But Peter was not out. He was qualified. This is how God works. He chooses weak vessels and makes them strong so others can see Jesus in us. Christ is our strength. It was Peter who Christ said He would build His Church upon.

> "He said to them, 'But who do you say that I am?' Simon Peter replied, 'You are the Christ, the Son of the living God.' And Jesus answered him, 'Blessed are you, Simon Bar-Jonah! For flesh and blood has not revealed this to you, but my Father who is in heaven. And I tell you, you are Peter, and on this rock I will build my church, and the gates

> of hell shall not prevail against it'" (Matthew 16:15-18, ESV).

God breaks through our mindsets with revelation as we ask Him too. We don't have to stay bound in a mindset of doubt. Sometimes fighting a doubtful mindset requires simply making a choice.

Trigger 4: Indecisiveness

Choosing one thing means saying no to something else. Not choosing is still choosing. At times the finality of our decisions delays us from choosing in the first place. We can be paralyzed by the thought of making a poor decision. We might doubt our ability to choose rightly, but in the end, we will be frozen in the doubtful mindset until we recognize our need to commit to a faithful mindset. There is no such thing as staying neutral.

Trigger 5: Fear of Failure

Failure is inevitable. Just ask Peter. But failure did not define him, nor does it define us. It just refines us as we press on to be more like Christ. We marvel at Thomas Edison for all his inventions, but what if failure had stopped him? We would not even recognize his name today.

Working on the incandescent lamp in 1879, Edison was not afraid of failure. He is a good example of what faithfulness looks like even when failure abounds.

Edison purportedly relentlessly searched everywhere for the best filament material but believed he would be successful. Yet those who worked with him were not so convinced.

Edison did not just display a positive attitude. He studied and believed. This shaped his mindset. In Edison's estimation he wasn't a failure, he just found a myriad of ways that did not work.

Do you see his mindset at work? Failure is not a stop sign, just a redirection. All we do develops us as we undergo sanctification in this life. Nothing defines us other than Christ. Whatever we are called to do in this life is an offering to Jesus as we do it with all our might—and a lot of might is required.

Maybe the failure in your life is personal—a failed marriage or failure in parenting. All failure is covered by the blood of Jesus. We don't have to be afraid anymore. Fear is a common theme of all the mindsets. It inhibits us and causes us to stay bound in mindsets that direct our lives away from God. But God can unlock our mindsets and set us free.

Learning to Trust Again

The word "believe" occurs 267 times in various translations of Scripture.[18] Most of those usages were by Jesus. Jesus encountered doubt again and again. Doubt is a big deal as it prevents us from seeing the truth and living it out. Here are some tips to strengthen our belief muscle:

Tip 1: Faith

Faith is a fight. Initially, Christ told us simply to believe. That is all the work that is required for salvation. However, walking our salvation out every day is a battle as the enemy wants to undermine our faith. If he can break through our belief system and get us to choose lesser mindsets, we will be unproductive in our walk with God.

We must fight doubt with faith. It will certainly be a fight, friend, but will be so worth it. "And without faith it is impossible to please him, for whoever would draw near to God must believe that he exists and that he rewards those who seek him" (Hebrews 11:6, ESV).

Tip 2: Hope

Hope is not hope if it is dependent upon a certain outcome. Doubt happens because we place our hope in things that cannot deliver. "For in this hope we were saved. Now hope that is seen is not hope. For who hopes for what he sees? But if we hope for what we do not see, we wait for it with patience" (Romans 8:24-25, ESV). The doubtful mindset longs for things in this world. But placing our hope in Christ leaves no room for doubt.

Tip 3: Trust

Those of us who attend different group events have surely participated in the trust-fall exercise. I've never been good at this game where each participant falls backward trusting some random person to prevent her from hitting the floor. First, my poor partner doesn't know how much I really weigh—and won't! Second, these events never allow for a practice session. And third, I am not much of a risk-taker, especially with someone I don't know. But trust in God is different. It is not blind faith.

God has proven His character, and His promises never fail. To trust God, we must choose to ditch the doubtful mindset. This means letting go of what we are holding on to. Trust isn't trust if we have any doubt. Relying on our own judgment prevents us from relying on God's. When in doubt, we must leave it out and embrace God's ways even when they don't seem to make sense.

Tip 4: Believe in God's Goodness

Doubt arises sometimes because life does not always go exactly the way we think it should. In such moments can we still believe God is good? Why is God's goodness important? When we begin to doubt, God's goodness is a benchmark for our faith. We know we can trust Him because we know His character.

Sometimes we judge God's goodness on whether life feels good to us in the moment. During times of suffering, we can feel betrayed by God, especially when we are living as faithful disciples of Christ. But we must be careful to weed out our entitlement attitude.

Evil happens in this world. And the presence of evil can cause the absence of faith if we do not understand evil in light of the cross. Evil does not get the last word, praise God. Our good God saw us in our sin and set His love on us. He had every right to condemn us, but He condemned Himself instead.

What a good, good God. He is holy and perfect; we are not. But He loves us anyway. When we struggle to trust God, we need to explore His promises to debunk the doubts of a good, perfect God. Doubt the doubts, not God.

Tip 5: Fleece

It's OK to dip our toes into the water to see if it is safe before we make a decision. We might be used to our old mindset, and a shift in our thoughts might be scary. Gideon used a fleece to discern God's will (Judges 6:37). We should not check our brains at the door as we go through life. We should ask God what right thinking is and use a fleece if necessary. God's Word is ready to help us filter out what belongs to the carnal mindset so we can think like Christ.

Getting to the Root

Those of us with a doubtful mindset have been scorched a time or two by life's circumstances, leaving it difficult for us to commit. But the faithfulness of Christ can restore our doubtful mindset to one of faith. Pain in this life does not mean God does not care. We can choose to adopt a mindset of faith by the grace of Christ. Jesus shows us how.

Mindset of Christ

Christ willingly chose to be subjected to temptation in the desert. Physically weak and hungry, Satan tried his best to get Christ to doubt God the Father and to submit to a different mindset. Satan even used the Word of God in his arsenal. But Christ knew the Word of God and used it to refute the lies.

> "Then the devil took him to the holy city and set him on the pinnacle of the temple and said to him, 'If you are the Son of God, throw yourself down, for it is written, "He will command his angels concerning you," and "On their hands they will bear you up, lest you strike your foot against a stone."' Jesus said to him, 'Again it is written, "You shall not put the Lord your God to the test"' (Matthew 4:5-7, ESV).

The enemy is the source of all our doubt. He injects doubt with the little word "if." Satan tried to get Jesus to doubt His very identity and to use His divine power rather than to walk in His humanity. But Jesus did not give in to the doubtful mindset. He walked in faith and showed us how to rely on the

Word of God when doubt creeps in. When we are tempted to doubt, we can go to God's Word just like Jesus did.

Mind Renewal: Keys to Unlock Our Mind

Key Thought:

Don't doubt in the dark what God reveals in the light.

Key Verse: Truth from God's Word.

"But let him ask in faith, with no doubting, for the one who doubts is like a wave of the sea that is driven and tossed by the wind" (James 1:6, ESV).

Key Change: Application—Releasing Doubt and Increasing Faith.

Write down all your doubts in your journal. Ask yourself for the source behind those doubts, then search for Scriptures to help you speak faith to those doubts. Pray and ask God to help increase your faith (Luke 17:5). Jesus will do it. We only need faith as small as a mustard seed for it to grow.

Counselor's Corner

Doubt robs us of our confidence and keeps us at a standstill. Those of us who struggle with doubt can be helped mightily by learning a weekly promise of God. As we stockpile these verses in our minds, we will have new positive declarations to reflect upon regularly.

I work with clients who don't know God's Word well enough to recite His encouraging words to themselves when life hits hard. Or, like me, they often forget what they know to be true. Walking in faith and overcoming doubt requires creating a systematic approach to remembering God's promises and goodness.

There are easy ways to keep God's Word in front of us. I recently stepped inside a friend's bathroom and saw her daily calendar. The Scripture posted there was just what I needed that day. I smiled and silently thanked God for the gentle reminder. The late Billy Graham would place open Bibles all over his home. He saw them as opportunities to feed on spiritual nourishment like soul snacks throughout the day. Similarly, I've placed devotionals in almost every room of my home. We can display Bible verses and words of encouragement on our walls. A close friend purchased an image of a female warrior to remind herself that she is in a battle that God has already won. When the visual reminders of God's truth we've displayed in our homes become overlooked, we can relocate these biblical reminders, find new ones, or make it our intention to study them anew.

Being intentional about surrounding ourselves with people who believe in the goodness of God also reinforces our faith. I see this as a major role of a Christian counselor. Each week, I remind my clients of the truths the enemy negates through life circumstances.

When friends don't call us back immediately, it doesn't make us any less important or lovable. When we experience one loss after another, it doesn't mean God has forgotten about us. Sometimes negative life scripts begin to get chiseled into our spirits, and we need an outside perspective to remind us of our God-given heritage.

This perspective doesn't have to come from a counselor. We can also gather a team of women in our lives to lift our spirits, remind us of God's promises, and affirm our life purpose. Such a tribe will help us to overcome our doubts and propel us forward.

Taking action energizes us and shrinks the doubts that plague us. Movement demands faith, and one small step can build on another. Starting with small steps keeps us from feeling overwhelmed. When we feel like we can't even get out of bed, if we can just move far enough to wash our face and brush our teeth, momentum will take it from there. These small actions seem doable.

I do this with writing. I love speaking and inspiring people face-to-face, but staring at a screen for hours is not my favorite task. When I want to avoid work, I tell myself just to write 500 words. Along the way, I remember my "why," and that motivates me. When our why is more important to us than our doubts, we will move past the internal obstacles holding us back. Faith can move mountains (Matthew 17:20), but I find with most of us faith means taking one step at a time with a team of people by our side.

How about you? What are you doubting you can do today? How can you remind yourself of the promises God has given you? Who could you call who has witnessed His work in your life? What baby step could you take today as you move in faith?

Mindset Movement: *Buy a daily calendar or devotional, download a printable, or write God's promises for you on some sticky notes. Then place them in prominent places where you can see them often.*

Chapter Seven

The Helpless Mindset—Battling Apathy and Weakness

> "Likewise the Spirit helps us in our weakness. For we do not know what to pray for as we ought, but the Spirit himself intercedes for us with groanings too deep for words. And he who searches hearts knows what is the mind of the Spirit, because the Spirit intercedes for the saints according to the will of God."
>
> —Romans 8:26-27, ESV

"God won't give you more than you can bear."

"You are strong. God knew you could handle this."

Don't we love statements like these? Wait, what's that? Haven't we also uttered these words to some poor soul? Probably. Maybe we didn't say these exact words, but the sentiment was close enough.

I confess I am not very appreciative when these token statements above are spoken to me, but I have dished out my share of these trite expressions, too. Sometimes we just don't have the appropriate words to help someone who seems helpless. So we throw some well-meaning words out just hoping they will resonate and provide comfort. But when we feel hopeless ourselves, we feel the emptiness of these words that are void of theological backing.

God's Word is our comfort. Man's words, well, they fall short. And sometimes we just need to give people Jesus when life feels overwhelming.

When Life Is More Than We Can Handle

Polite advice aside, how do we handle life when it is too much for us to handle? Paul found himself in such a situation.

> "We do not want you to be uninformed, brothers and sisters, about the troubles we experienced in the province of Asia. We were under great pressure, far beyond our ability to endure, so that we despaired of life itself. Indeed, we felt we had received the sentence of death. But this happened that we might not rely on ourselves but on God, who raises the dead. He has delivered us from such a deadly peril, and he will deliver us again. On him we have set our hope that he will continue to deliver us, as you help us by your prayers. Then many will give thanks on our behalf for the gracious favor granted us in answer to the prayers of many" (2 Corinthians 1:8-11, NIV).

Paul was in a dire situation indeed—far beyond his ability to handle, to the point of thinking he was going to die. But

God delivered Paul. And Paul was confident God would do it again.

Notice, Paul did not hope to avoid such times. He did not say "if" he was ever helpless again. Paul wrote that God "will" continue to deliver him again and again. Helplessness is a part of life. However, the times when we are helpless reveal where our true hope lies, and I might add, those times reveal our grit as well. No one volunteers to be placed in a helpless situation, but then, with Christ we are never truly helpless. It all depends on our mindset.

When Helplessness Becomes a Mission

There is something really humbling about being so weak we cannot take care of ourselves. We don't like asking for help. Why is that? Stinkin' pride. Helping others is gratifying, but others helping us is just embarrassing. We are supposed to have our act together. But perhaps times of helplessness help us regain a truth: None of us really have our act together. We are all desperately in need before our Holy Savior. We tend to forget that.

One of my biggest struggles with helplessness involves my health. Autoimmune issues have made me feel so inferior and weak, and well, I will say it—helpless. Just before my sixth bout with pneumonia, I could feel it coming on, and I knew I was in trouble. The doctors could not figure out what kind of pneumonia it was and did not know how to treat it. None of the multiple antibiotics they dumped into me were working, and I began to experience kidney failure. My body was so weak I could hardly walk to the bathroom.

In the silence of my hospital room, I cried out to God for help. As I admitted my need, I sensed God asking me if He could use me in that place.

"Here?" I asked in my spirit. "I can barely speak, but God, here I am. Send me."

Gently the Holy Spirit nudged me to do my devotions and to write a Scripture on the white board. Friends, it took all my energy to do this, but our sweet Savior showed me then that our moments of helplessness are a mission if we accept it. God wants to use our moments of helplessness as an example to those around us. The rain falls on both the good and the bad. All of us will bear a little rain. How we bear it can impact others with the Gospel.

As the nurses came to take care of me, one by one asked about the verses I wrote on the board. Then one nurse said, "Ma'am, you need to get up and walk. You need to fight."

Over the next week I slowly started walking, and on each walk, God began to give me assignments: "Give your flowers away to the others on this hall."

Once all my hospital gifts had been given away, the Holy Spirit whispered, "Give them your music." I had recordings from my music ministry for such a time as this.

Y'all, I was not a pretty sight slowly creeping down the hall in two hospital gowns (to cover the openings in the gowns), using a walker and an oxygen tank. But it's funny how in our helplessness, if we take the focus off our condition and consider it a mission, we can find incredible joy.

As I struggled to walk, I got stronger. God healed me in more than one way during that hospital stay. In my final moments there, one of my nurses came into the room: "I just want you to know I have rededicated my life to Jesus because of watching you during your illness."

Wow. When I think this could have been a missed opportunity if I had given into the helpless mindset, it makes me weep. All around us people are truly spiritually helpless. We must help them, even and especially in our helplessness.

In Our Weaknesses, We Are Strong

We don't want to admit we are weak, but when we own up to it, it brings relief if we know where to find help. Being helpless might be the strongest position we have. When we don't know how to have the mind of Christ, we can simply come to God. The Holy Spirit intercedes on our behalf. We were never supposed to be strong enough on our own in the first place. When it leads us to relying on Christ's strength, not ours, admitting our weakness is our secret inner strength.

Still, pain can discourage us, and we don't sometimes see a way out. We may think no one understands what we are going through and put on a victim's mindset or a mindset of spiritual apathy, thinking we just don't care anymore. We can feel forgotten because we cannot escape our suffering. However, sometimes escaping a situation does not free us like we thought it would. The good news is being helpless is not a sin. In fact, recognizing our helplessness is a sign of humility that can rescue us.

The Secret of Abiding

There is a secret refuge for those willing to search for it. Many who rely on their own strength will not find it. This refuge is for those who admit their need for help, and it is found by abiding in Christ. "I am the vine; you are the branches. Whoever abides in me and I in him, he it is that bears much fruit, for apart from me you can do nothing" (John 15:5, ESV).

Apart from Christ we can do nothing. That sounds helpless, doesn't it? Yet those who abide in Christ are not frantic in their helplessness. They don't have the helpless mindset. They have a Helper to enable them in their time of need.

God Sends a Helper

I love that the Holy Spirit has the nickname "Helper." God knows our helplessness, friend. We don't have to have the helpless mindset though because God sent us a Helper. How will He help us?

- **He is with us.** "And I will ask the Father, and he will give you another Helper, to be with you forever" (John 14:16, ESV).
- **He guides us.** "When the Spirit of truth comes, he will guide you into all the truth …" (John 16:13a, ESV).
- **He teaches us.** "But the Helper, the Holy Spirit, whom the Father will send in my name, he will teach you all things and bring to your remembrance all that I have said to you" (John 14:26, ESV).
- **He bears witness about Jesus.** "But when the Helper comes, whom I will send to you from the Father, the Spirit of truth, who proceeds from the Father, he will bear witness about me" (John 15:26, ESV).
- **He gives us gifts.** "It is the one and only Spirit who distributes all these gifts. He alone decides which gift each person should have" (1 Corinthians 12:11, NLT).

- **He prays for us.** "And he who searches hearts knows what is the mind of the Spirit, because the Spirit intercedes for the saints according to the will of God" (Romans 8:27, ESV).
- **He gives us hope.** "May the God of hope fill you with all joy and peace in believing, so that by the power of the Holy Spirit you may abound in hope" (Romans 15:13, ESV).
- **He sets us free.** "Now the Lord is the Spirit, and where the Spirit of the Lord is, there is freedom" (2 Corinthians 3:17, ESV). This includes freedom from negative mindsets, friends.
- **He helps us bear godly fruit.** "But the fruit of the Spirit is love, joy, peace, patience, kindness, goodness, faithfulness, gentleness, self-control; against such things there is no law" (Galatians 5:22-23, ESV).
- **He gives us words to say.** "For the Holy Spirit will teach you at that time what you should say" (Luke 12:12, NIV).
- **He gives us confidence**. "And when they had prayed … they were all filled with the Holy Spirit and continued to speak the word of God with boldness" (Acts 4:31, ESV).
- **He secures our salvation.** "In him you also, when you heard the word of truth, the gospel of your salvation, and believed in him, were sealed with the promised Holy Spirit" (Ephesians 1:13, ESV).
- **He helps us believe.** "So I want you to know that no one speaking by the Spirit of God will curse Jesus, and no one can say Jesus is Lord, except by the Holy Spirit" (1 Corinthians 12:3, NLT).

- **He empowers the weak.** "But you will receive power when the Holy Spirit has come upon you, and you will be my witnesses in Jerusalem and in all Judea and Samaria, and to the end of the earth" (Acts 1:8, ESV).
- **He reveals.** "When the Spirit of truth comes … whatever he hears he will speak, and he will declare to you the things that are to come" (John 16:13, ESV).
- **He heals and comforts us.** "The LORD sustains him on his sickbed; in his illness you restore him to full health" (Psalm 41:3, ESV).

How beautiful. Our sweet Holy Spirit, our Comforter sustains us. He was there in the beginning of time, and He is with those who obey God to the end. "And we are witnesses to these things, and so is the Holy Spirit, whom God has given to those who obey him" (Acts 5:32, ESV).

I am sure my list is not complete, but you get the point. When Jesus said He was sending a Helper, He was sending us all we would need for this life. We are not helpless, friend. We just need to ask for help from our Helper. Yet despite having the Holy Spirit, sometimes we can take matters into our own hands.

Good in a Crisis

Sometimes we feel helpless because of momentary crises—at least that's how high-pressured situations affect me quite often. One year when we had an earthquake, I had no idea what was happening. (Earthquakes are rare where I live.) The entire house was shaking, and dishes were flying out of the cabinet. I first thought a dually truck was revving its engine in our driveway. But when my bed started shaking, my son and I looked at one another and realized it was an earthquake.

I told my children to run with me to the basement. Then I realized that was a bad idea. Then I told them to run with me to the garage. Yep, another bad idea. Then I suggested we run outside. Freak-out mode puts me in a helpless mindset pretty darn quick. However, one Old Testament heroine, Abigail, provides a great example of how we can handle what seems like a hopeless situation without freaking out.

Lessons from Abby: What's a Girl to Do?

Abigail was married to Nabal, *a fool*, his name's literal meaning. Scripture says Nabal was rich, harsh, badly behaved, worthless in general (1 Samuel 25), and an abusive husband to Abigail specifically. One day Nabal's foolishness nearly cost the lives of his men's and his own. When David asked Nabal for food for him and his 400 soldiers—an overwhelming request, no doubt—Nabal flat-out refused despite David's protection of Nabal's men. This insulted David, causing him to prepare to decimate Nabal and his men for the inhospitable response. But the cool and steady response of Abigail rescued the day. Let's see how one woman not giving into helplessness saved countless lives.

When word got out about David's pending attack upon Nabal and his army, a young man came and informed Abigail. First, Abigail must have had a capable reputation for a man to approach her about a matter of warfare.

Second, Abigail was not slow in her response. She did not give in to the drama of the moment but got busy doing what she could. In this instance, that meant she started cooking.

Third, the Bible says Abigail was a discerning woman. She did not tell her husband her plan as she went to feed David and his men. She knew Nabal would have a foolish and possibly abusive response.

Fourth, Abigail was humble as she approached David, taking responsibility for her husband's actions.

Fifth, her wise response to David saved her life and the lives of all her household. David acknowledged her for it: "And David said to Abigail, 'Blessed be the Lord, the God of Israel, who sent you this day to meet me! Blessed be your discretion, and blessed be you, who have kept me this day from bloodguilt and from working salvation with my own hand'" (1 Samuel 25:32-33, ESV).

Abigail missed an opportunity for a big pity party. She could have been paralyzed with fear because of the very real threat of David and his army. She could have been immobilized by feelings of futility because of her marriage to a fool. But Abigail did not give in to the helpless mindset. She chose to walk in wisdom rather than fear and to be diligent in her response.

We have much we can learn from Abigail. Sometimes in our helpless estate we need to get busy focused on a solution rather than just giving up.

The Helpless One's God

Still at other times, Scripture talks about those who are truly helpless—legitimate victims of wicked people. What then? The weak have power from on high. "He gives power to the weak and strength to the powerless" (Isaiah 40:29, NLT).

Sometimes in our helplessness we can feel invisible to God because it seems like He does not act soon enough on our behalf. The wicked appear to be able to harm the helpless unchecked. But God sees, friend. And He is our Helper. The One who is supreme over all became a servant of those He sought to help. He went to extremes to rescue His beloved and became helpless Himself to save the helpless.

Trigger 1: Relying on Man

"It is better to take refuge in the LORD than to trust in man" (Psalm 118:8, ESV). Regarding the opinion of man is a stumbling block, for sure—especially when we go to man for help instead of God. Relationship troubles abound when we enable one another to seek help from everywhere else rather than turn to the strength only God provides.

Time and again God's people went to idols or foreign nations for help rather than God. "Woe to those who go down to Egypt for help, who rely on horses, who trust in the multitude of their chariots and in the great strength of their horsemen, but do not look to the Holy One of Israel, or seek help from the LORD" (Isaiah 31:1, NIV). God wants to be our help.

Trigger 2: Relying on Self

Our pride can be the biggest problem we have. So many times we won't ask for help because of pride. We are all probably familiar with people who will not accept help because it somehow demeans them. But unless we admit our need of God, we will indeed remain helpless.

God receives the glory when we rely on Him. When we rely on self, we show our desire to be glory hogs. Those who recognize their sufficiency is in Christ alone are freed from the helpless mindset. They don't put false confidence in their own strength. They know where their help comes from. "Not that we are sufficient in ourselves to claim anything as coming from us, but our sufficiency is from God" (2 Corinthians 3:5, ESV).

Trigger 3: Reality

At times life can be overwhelming. This truth can provoke a helpless mindset. When all we do is contemplate our difficult reality rather than God's ability, we find ourselves in a helpless mindset.

The realist looks at circumstances and does not see a way out. But the person of faith looks at circumstances and sees an opportunity. The reality is God is greater than any problem we face. And He wants to help us. "For I, the LORD your God, hold your right hand; it is I who say to you, 'Fear not, I am the one who helps you'" (Isaiah 41:13, ESV).

Trigger 4: Focus

Just focusing on the problems at hand enlarges them in our eyes. But focusing on God's power and care reminds us we aren't meant to bear our troubles alone. "Cast all your anxiety on him because he cares for you" (1 Peter 5:7, NIV). One way to do this is to look at God's promises and then His fulfillment of them. Focusing on His goodness and His character while we study God's Word increases our faith in God's ability and desire to help us.

Trigger 5: Despair

Helplessness can become despair when we give up looking for a rescue or trusting in God. We give ourselves over to our helplessness rather than giving our helplessness over to God. When my children were growing up, one of our favorite movies was *Anne of Green Gables*. All of Anne's histrionics made us laugh. Everything was melodramatic. Yet secretly we could relate to her and perhaps wished we could express ourselves like she did.

In one scene, Anne Shirley was trying to figure out why Marilla was not given to the helpless mindset.

Anne Shirley: Can't you even imagine you're in the depths of despair?

Marilla Cuthbert: No, I cannot. To despair is to turn your back on God.[19]

Well said, Marilla. Despair says we are too far gone for help, that our circumstance is impossible, even to God. Even though God is in complete control, all-powerful and all-knowing, our despair blinds us to this reality.

Still, there is a part of us that despairs because God does not seem to be doing anything. What then? When we bear our suffering well for God's glory, we might see our despair transformed into hope that no longer views our circumstances the same way.

Finding Strength

As I sat before ten people staring at me during a job interview, the infamous interview question came up: What are your strengths? The Holy Spirit moved in my soul. "I have none, except Christ—He is my strength."

The words burned in my soul as I spoke them. Of course! Why had I not realized this before? There's always so much pressure to perform and be strong, but abiding is the secret.

And Christ, He *is* my strength—even if I don't always live into that reality. Here are some tips to help us do that.

Tip 1: Refocus

If we can see our helpless situation in light of eternity, what seems dire now will not be so tomorrow or five years from now. When we reframe what seems helpless, we are no longer hopeless. As we refocus, we can see our problems in view of God's sovereignty and purposes rather than ours.

Tip 2: Acceptance

Sometimes we remain in a state of helplessness because we become entrenched with bad attitudes that just make us more helpless. But there is something beautiful about accepting our situation. That's right. Acceptance does not mean we don't care. It means we do.

When we accept our situation with joy, we show our care about God's glory more than our comfort. We choose to acknowledge that our helplessness allows God to accomplish more than just helping us. He is also helping others around us. Our struggle is not just about us. How we accept our struggles in life is a witness to others. And as we walk with Jesus through the struggle, our character transforms to be more like Christ's.

Tip 3: Find Our Strength

God promised never to leave or forsake us. He has provided us with everything we need in Christ Jesus. Accessing Christ as our strength might mean searching His Word for help. And it might mean discovering strengths within that we have not recognized before.

It has been said necessity is the mother of invention. It is not until we are in a place of need or helplessness that we recognize we have been needy all along. All we have has been given to us. When weakness peeks through, it is an opportunity to dig deep and find the strength only God provides.

Tip 4: Find a Solution

We don't find a solution by sitting around bemoaning our situation. We might need to admit our need, which is humbling to do, and God might want to use someone to provide for us. After my ex-husband and I separated, and it was just my five children and I, we were in a pretty helpless situation. But helpless situations are where we see God provide. If we don't encounter times of need, we cannot understand how blessed we are. Countless times God met my family's needs, often through miraculous means. My attempts to find a solution at times were thwarted, but then God made a way.

Tip 5: Rely on God

"Some trust in chariots and some in horses, but we trust in the name of the Lord our God" (Psalm 20:7, ESV). When all else fails, rely on God. Actually, we would save ourselves much sorrow if we would just start with God. How do we do that?

R – Remember what He has done and who He is.

E – Examine His Word and our hearts.

L – Look to Him in prayer, not to our own solutions.

Y – Yield to His plan, not ours.

Getting to the Root

Admitting our need hurts. But not admitting it does, too. Helplessness is not helpless unless we let it be. Acknowledging our need can be a beautiful moment of finding and applying Christ as our strength. Christ showed us how to find strength when we feel so very helpless.

Mindset of Christ

When Christ was seemingly helpless, He could have called a legion of angels to help Him, but He didn't. Joy was His refuge. Christ chose to focus on the joy set before Him, even as He was tortured. He saw that good would come out of His suffering because God promised it would, and God never fails us. The Greek noun for joy, *kara,* is not just a passive emotion but can be descriptive of a condition of the soul; emphasized by the expression "to fill with joy."[20] According to the *Theological Dictionary of the New Testament,* "Joy is not just inward. It is a disposition of the whole man. … Joy is native to God alone. It is found only in God."[21] Christ had complete joy even as He was being crucified—deep, abiding joy that's found in God alone.

In their helplessness, people try to find delight in things to cure their pain rather than in God, who they were made for. The thought of Christ being filled with joy even as He suffered cruelly, carrying His cross, is amazing. Even a splinter can ruin my day sometimes if I let it. But Christ chose helplessness and the most extreme pain to redeem our souls. And in that place of suffering, He fixed His mind on something higher: God's purposes in the pain. We can, too. When we feel helpless to carry our own crosses, Christ shows us how.

Mind Renewal: Keys to Unlock Our Mind

Key Thought:

The greatest helplessness we have has been provided for.

Key Verse: Truth from God's Word

"When we were utterly helpless, Christ came at just the right time and died for us sinners" (Romans 5:6, NLT).

Key Change: Application—Finding Help in the Right Place

What do you feel powerless or helpless to change? Give it to God, friend. Jot down in your journal the helpless situations or relationships and ask God for His perspective. Sometimes when we reframe our pain, we discover we are no longer helpless.

Counselor's Corner

After returning from back-to-back trips to Switzerland and Arizona, where I spent time climbing mountains in both places, I knew something was seriously wrong with my left hip. I wasn't even 50 yet, and I received the bad news I needed a new one. Recovering from a total hip replacement required me to retrain weak muscles. To do so, I needed to do two things: (1) focus intently on getting stronger each day; and (2) set aside time for repetitive strength exercises.

Intentional focus and mundane repetition are also two factors to overcome what counselors call "learned helplessness." My doctor set up appointments with a physical therapist for me because he knew that as good as my intentions were, I wouldn't faithfully do the necessary exercises without a designated time, place, and person to hold me accountable.

For my clients who are serious about embracing stronger thoughts about themselves, a commitment to weekly counseling or coaching sessions empowers them to build stronger neuropathways in their brains similar to the way a physical therapist helps someone build stronger muscles to support their movement. At the end of almost every session, I ask my clients to set a SMART goal—specific, measurable, attainable, realistic, and timely. They tell me what they are going to do, when and where they are going to do it, and for how long.

When setting goals, the tough part for most of us is being realistic. Setting unrealistic goals and failing to achieve them reinforces hopelessness and makes us more likely to quit. We need to make our goals almost too easy so we set ourselves up for success. Achieving our goals with the help of God and others teaches us that we can create change. Celebrating minor achievements creates positive energy and momentum. We need positive reinforcement when we are feeling helpless because we are naturally wired to avoid pain, seek pleasure, and conserve energy.

Learned helplessness is created by how we interact with life circumstances and negative people in our lives. We can speak empowering words out loud to counteract these messages. During some sessions my clients role-play standing in truth while I become their negative mindset who says things like:

- "What makes you think you could ever do something like that?"
- "Do you really think you are smart enough?"
- "You can't even run your home. How could you ever run a business?"

When we hear words like these, it's important to refute them in our minds. However, it's even more empowering to say our truth out loud. My clients practice until they can say confident responses like these:

- "I know this is what God is calling me to do, and I trust Him to work through me. I've had several people say I'd be really good at this."
- "I am smart and have prepared myself well. I may still need to learn some things, but everyone does. I know I can figure it out."
- "I may be a lousy housekeeper, but I'm a great decorator. The job descriptions aren't the same. When I'm doing something I really love, I've always been successful."

Now it's your turn. What "life muscles" do you want to strengthen so you can overcome feelings of helplessness? Currently, for me, it's meal planning and making better food choices. To give me time and space to accomplish this goal, I'm following my own advice by working with a nutritionist.

Her first plan for me seemed amazing, but within a couple of days I realized it wasn't realistic in the middle of a book deadline. We adapted and spread out the changes over a longer period. Even though I am struggling and tempted to quit, I am not giving up. Every time we start again or do a little more, it is still progress.

Finally, we can't forget we always have the ultimate power source available. In the Gospel of John, Jesus said He is the vine, and we are the branches (John 15:5). We must not forget to tap into the power of God by praying to Him for help. I beg Him to help me resist temptation (James 4:7). I ask Him to give me strength to overcome my weaknesses (2 Corinthians 12:10). Finally, I ask God to allow me to accept my weaknesses—not so I remain helpless, but so I know the way forward is through my connection with Him.

Mindset Movement 1: *Write out a SMART goal for your life this week and share it with someone.*

Mindset Movement 2: *Write out and practice your response for the next time someone says something negative that makes you doubt yourself. Then you will be prepared to speak words of truth that negate the negativity and increase your confidence.*

Chapter Eight

The Hurried Mindset—Battling Overcommitment and Margin

"Desire without knowledge is not good, and whoever makes haste with his feet misses his way."
—Proverbs 19:2, ESV

"Hurry, we're gonna be late!"

If I had a nickel for every time someone in my family has said that statement, truly, I would be a wealthy woman. I really did not want to pass on the traits of running late and rushing around to my children. But try as I might, I still set that pattern. Frankly, it must be in the genes because several of my kids exhibit these traits.

The hurried mindset makes sense to me. Time is too precious to waste. Being efficient with our time means we get more out of every minute of life. Even my dad would rise between 3 or 4 in the morning to get more out of his day. I'm a chip off the ol' block.

My past life hack was to leave for my destination either right on time or late within five minutes. I reasoned no one is ready on time anyway, so punctuality was wasted effort. Being on time seemed almost heroic to me until someone told me this: "If you're on time, you're late." Busted. I cringed at the words. The bar was raised, and I did not want to meet it.

We live in a fast-paced society, and I admit the hurried mindset is one I can struggle with the most—except the word "struggle" may be overstating it a bit. At least I *think* about struggling with it. We give kudos to folks when they are busy. Being industrious beats sitting on a couch eating bonbons and watching soaps, hands down. But what is driving all this busyness?

Haste Makes Waste

Ever wonder about the saying, "Haste makes waste"? How can rushing around trying to save time actually waste it? One would think we could salvage time when we hurry, but maybe that's not true. What are we wasting with all this hasting? For one, rushing leads to mistakes. It can also cause friction in relationships. Most importantly, hurrying through life can cause us to miss the gift of the present.

Some Lessons from a Wise Guy

Solomon had some counsel for us Type A personalities, who incidentally are probably proud of that nickname, right? I mean, an A can't be bad, can it? Well, it can be if we don't know when to stop.

Solomon said, "One who hurries his footsteps errs" (Proverbs 19:2b, NASB). The word for hurries is the Hebrew word *'ûwts*, and it means "to urge, to press or to be pressed, to hasten or make haste, be narrow."[22] This verb is used four times in the Old Testament, each time in context of discouraging hasty words or actions.[23] What's the big deal about being hasty? Well, other than the fact the verse above indicates it can lead us to sin, hurriedness can cause many problems we might not readily see. Being hasty can cause us to live pressure-filled lives that lead to poor decisions. Also, a pressed mind can cause a narrow mindset, preventing us from seeing the bigger picture.

My husband has the reputation of being unflappable. As I rush around to get out the door, it's not a little irritating to see him remain in his one mode: S-L-O-W. (He would say *deliberate*). God has a sense of humor, doesn't He, hitching the tortoise and the hare together? However, I realize my husband holds a secret: He does not have a hurried mindset nor is he anxious. My spouse is not pushed by time or demands, and as a result he stays in control of his behavior. In short, he is a peaceful person.

My husband says it does not add to his life to become hurried, and he isn't responsible for other people's lateness. He made a cognitive decision, as Solomon suggested in the first half of Proverbs 19:2, "It is not good for a person to be without knowledge, And one who hurries his footsteps errs" (NASB). The word knowledge means discernment, wisdom, or understanding, but when combined with the word "without," it means ignorant or unaware.[24] We can be without knowledge when we rush around, letting panic consume us. But when we think our actions through, we might slow our pace down, realizing the hurried mindset should be reserved for dire situations, not everyday life.

The Cost of Rushing

Evidently there is a name for the crazed, hurried mindset. Who knew? I guess I was too busy to know about it. Cardiologists Meyer Friedman and Ray Rosenman coined the term "hurry sickness" and define it as "a continuous struggle and unremitting attempt to accomplish or achieve more and more things or participate in more and more events in less and less time."[25] The cost of getting more done in less time is not worth the price we pay, friends. We pay with our health, our relationships, and our quality of life.

The Bible tells us to count the costs before we build. "But don't begin until you count the cost. For who would begin construction of a building without first calculating the cost to see if there is enough money to finish it" (Luke 14:28, NLT). John Ortberg in his book *The Life You've Always Wanted* wrote that hurrying is a state of our heart. "Hurry is not just a disordered schedule. Hurry is a disordered heart."[26]

What's the Rush?

When my third daughter was little, she tended to run everywhere. When she needed to go to the kitchen, *thump, thump, thump*. Silence. Then *thump, thump, thump* again as she ran to whatever was next. She was so excited to get to the next thing. Maybe some of us adults are like that, too. Sometimes we don't know why we do what we do. But motives matter.

Considering our "why" can help us recognize if we need to prune things in our lives. Sometimes our busyness is due to the need to provide. Even then, Solomon reminds us of the futility of merely pursuing wealth. "Do not toil to acquire wealth; be discerning enough to desist" (Proverbs 23:4, ESV). Sometimes our busyness is due to poor planning or maybe due to a perfectionist mentality that does not know when to quit. The list could go on and on. But the truth is, we don't have to be in rush mode. We choose to be.

Initially, the reason for our rushing around can be because we want to be people of our word; we want to be hard workers. But there is also a surprise element lurking there: shame. We don't want to bear the shame for being late or not living up to our word or having to admit we bit off more than we could chew. Sometimes behind all our rushing is anxiety, pushing us forward to do something faster, right away. This can have a detrimental effect on our health and on our relationships.

The Life Behind Multitasking

More is not always better. Sure, people can marvel at all we get done, but is that really the goal? Multitasking can create similar symptoms to ADHD. Moving from one thing to the next can cause us to become forgetful, and our thinking can become muddled.

The pace at which we multitask matters, too. A hurried mindset coupled with multitasking creates stress and can cause us to lose focus on what really matters. Having goals is good, but we lose the joy of working on those goals if they always have to be accomplished quickly and at the same time as other things. We can lose perspective as we crank out our accomplishments.

To what end are we toiling so hard? It might be our end. This sobering thought has caused me to restructure how I do life. I now give exercise a more consistent place in my schedule—healthy eating, too. What I once "did not have time for" I now view as necessary. I put work into proper priority, and I have loved ones tell me when I start to do too much at the same time. And friends, this is an area I still struggle with. But having people who can speak into my life helps me to see when my blind spots prevent me from seeing that I switched into a hurried mindset once again.

When we lead a life of multitasking, it feels like time manages us rather than us managing our time. It's OK to slow our pace, breathe deeply, and set boundaries so we don't stay in hyper mode. Jesus did one thing at a time. We can, too.

Just Say No

It will be hard to change the way we have done things, especially because we might like all we achieve by being busy. But as we let go of one spinning plate at a time, we can restructure our productivity. Habit changes are in order. Here are ten ways to restructure time so the hurried mindset does not take over our life:

- **Hang up.** We can leave the phone in another room. Truly, it is OK if people cannot reach us the moment they want to.
- **Set limits.** We can ditch the temptation to do more than one thing at a time. We can make a list of what we want

to accomplish then review it to see what we can delegate to others. We are not heroes if we can do it all.

- **Focus.** When we are working on one thing, we can resist the temptation to check our email or social media account. It can be a habit, can't it? We don't have to check all the places where people contact us. We can set times when we check what we need to check.
- **Control.** We don't have to let scrolling control us. We control it. It's OK to check social media, but we can limit the time and places where we do.
- **Step away.** We can create moments several times a day when we step away from work and go for walks, take deep-breathing breaks, listen to music, or do anything that rejuvenates us.
- **Reevaluate.** Life does have busier seasons. We just have to make sure those seasons don't become a lifestyle. I chose to work multiple jobs to help put my kids through college. But when they were out of college, I continued to work multiple jobs so I could pursue a master's degree. It was super hard, y'all. And now I am pursuing a doctorate degree, but I have built in times where I do not do school to provide breaks. My husband and I have also found a way to work side by side when we are both working on projects. Again, there are times when we may need to live in a pressure cooker of time for a while, but hopefully we can choose a better pace of life after that season.
- **Compartmentalize.** Sometimes we just have a lot to get done. We can compartmentalize different tasks to specific times on our schedule and choose not to think about them until their scheduled times.

- **Busier is not better.** We can intentionally slow down the pace of how we do things.
- **Make the most of each moment.** We can practice being fully present in each moment. Each day is a gift from God. Being conscious of this helps us to "Make the most of every opportunity in these evil days." (Ephesians 5:16, NLT).
- **Leave things undone**: We can't do it all. Something might get left undone, and that's OK. We can choose what God calls us to do each day.

Work Ethic

So does all this "slow down" mentality mean we slack off in our work? No way. But working hard and efficiently does not require a stress-filled, hasty mindset. "Whatever you do, work heartily, as for the Lord and not for men" (Colossians 3:23 ESV). I enjoy work, especially ministry work. I like to be efficient in my work so I can get more done. But sometimes it can be easy to have a good work ethic and cross boundaries, ending up as a workaholic. The hurried mindset can be dangerous, even when our work is ministry related. We can blur boundaries and simply not know when to quit. If we don't know when to stop, it could mean we may not be able to.

Addiction of Busyness

The hurried mindset can be addictive. Getting things done is initially energizing. But if we hurry through life, we might just miss it. Being present in life will mean we have to learn how to leave the hurried mindset behind and settle into a slower gear so we can enjoy what God has given and where

He has placed us. The Bible's Martha can show us what this looks like.

A Lesson from Martha

Poor Martha has gotten a bad rap over the years. Being diligent is a wonderful characteristic to have, but there are some lessons we can learn from Martha taking diligence too far:

> "Now as they went on their way, Jesus entered a village. And a woman named Martha welcomed him into her house. And she had a sister called Mary, who sat at the Lord's feet and listened to his teaching. But Martha was distracted with much serving. And she went up to him and said, 'Lord, do you not care that my sister has left me to serve alone? Tell her then to help me.' But the Lord answered her, 'Martha, Martha, you are anxious and troubled about many things, but one thing is necessary. Mary has chosen the good portion, which will not be taken away from her'" (Luke 10:38-42, ESV).

Let's be honest. Martha had it goin' on. She had the gift of hospitality. Check. She was diligent. Check. She had a servant's heart. Check. And she might have been a little OCD, not sure. But she was ready when guests came over.

However, when we take a closer look, the Bible says Martha was distracted with much serving. The word distracted is from the Greek word *perispáō*, which means "to be driven about mentally, to be over-occupied, too busy, to be cumbered."[27] This definition is eye-opening, isn't it? And a bit ironic. To be cumbered means "to reduce to idleness or inactivity."[28] So all our rushing around can actually make us ineffective. And the busyness of our minds can cause our minds to become focused on the negative. What began as beautiful service to Jesus and the others turned into bitter resentment for Martha.

Jesus saw Martha's mind was in overdrive, as her hurried mindset pushed her. Christ saw her thoughts. He sees ours, too. Notice this Scripture does not say serving is bad. Of course not! But it's the word "much" that reveals life was a little off-balance for Martha.

Sometimes when we want to serve people, we can worry too much about making things perfect instead of just enjoying their company. This degree of perfectionism led Martha to assign false motives to, well, Jesus. She assumed He didn't care that she was working harder than Mary. Comparison was robbing Martha of the reward for her service.

And Martha was wrong; Jesus did care. Jesus knew Martha's heart. He knew the real cause behind her actions. Martha was anxious and troubled about many things. Sometimes in the hurried mindset our thoughts go a mile a minute, and we think on negative things rather than slowing down—like my husband does—and thinking about what we are doing. Let's be clear: Mary was not just sitting around all the time, to be sure. But she knew her priorities, and no one was going to take Jesus out of her schedule. How about us?

Finding Balance in an Unbalanced World

Resting is not lazy and being busy is not necessarily diligent either. Finding balance in our lives is increasingly difficult with all the incessant demands in our social-media-driven world. When we are always only a phone call or text away, it is hard to find moments of calm. But we can learn how to function at a different speed. Decreasing the hidden triggers that feed the overcommitted lifestyle, we can learn a new approach for life.

Trigger 1: Perfectionism

It takes time to do things. And then it takes more time to do them perfectly. Perfectionism is overrated. I'm not saying we shouldn't give our very best, but sometimes we can make an idol out of perfect. Ultimately, our labor in the Lord should be for the Lord, not our glory. Sometimes we can forget that.

When we can't let go of something because it's not perfect, we get caught up in the hurried mindset. We need to B-R-E-A-T-H-E. Not to burst anyone's bubble, but we are not perfect. Obsessing about things being "just so" takes away from the joy of life. We can do good work, yes, and we can also be OK with revisions in their time.

Trigger 2: Judgment

Perhaps someone else is driving the hurried mindset within us. Maybe a boss grows accustomed to our productivity and doesn't want to settle for less. But more often we are our own worst taskmaster; we expect too much of ourselves. Or ironically, we might even be judged as a workaholic or out of balance.

Behind the curtain of harsh judgment is fear of man and perhaps idolatry. We want praise from others, and sometimes we feel our worth comes from high productivity. If people's praises encourage us, their judgment can make us feel "less than." However, our worth does not come from our work, and our worth does not come from how fast we work. We must not let judgment keep us bound in the hurried mindset.

Trigger 3: Worry

Why worry about time? We fear missing out on something. Or maybe we fear whether we have done enough. But hurrying around will not help us to measure up either. Still, the hurried mindset can be fueled by worry we heap on ourselves or deadlines of our own making. Jesus reminds us to keep our focus. When we put God first, everything else falls into place. "But seek first the kingdom of God and his righteousness, and all these things will be added to you. Therefore do not be anxious about tomorrow, for tomorrow will be anxious for itself. Sufficient for the day is its own trouble" (Matthew 6:33-34, ESV).

Trigger 4: Impatience

Hurry up! Get it done! Another driver behind the hurried mindset is impatience. We want it done NOW. Why? Impatience robs us of what can be gained in the process. The instant gratification mindset from our surrounding culture and our flesh encourages an impatient spirit. But the world will not end if something takes a little longer to accomplish. "And which of you by being anxious can add a single hour to his span of life?" (Matthew 6:27, ESV).

Trigger 5: Performance Mentality

A competitive spirit lies behind this contributor to the hurried mindset: performance mentality. We strive to be the best. Our competition may be with ourselves, or it may be against others. But what are we competing for? All this pushing to be the best is in vain because there never truly is a best. Jesus already took that spot. This does not mean I am an advocate for apathy either. But giving our best for Jesus does not mean burning out. Making time to be still before God actually helps us perform better. "Be still before the LORD and wait patiently for him; fret not yourself over the one who prospers in his way, over the man who carries out evil devices!" (Psalm 37:7, ESV).

Margin Matters

For much of my adult life I have lamented about not having enough time. But God gives us enough time to do His will. We choose what to do with the time He gives. This humbles me. I am so intent on wanting to do the will of God that sometimes I miss my need for rest. But there is a sweet place of rest when we pause to discern God's will, recognizing what is ours to do and what isn't. "And the world is passing away along with its desires, but whoever does the will of God abides forever" (1 John 2:17, ESV).

Sometimes we can also miss opportunities to do things well because we don't think we have enough time due to a perpetual hurried mindset. Every parent has likely had hurried children say they don't have time for chores, right? But we make time for what is important to us. There is balance to the removal of the hurried mindset. We do need to be diligent. Sometimes we just need a few reminders to help us get back on the right track again. Here are a few.

Tip 1: Detox

More is not better. Maybe we have subscribed to the hurried mindset for so long that we don't know how to unsubscribe. I sure wish it was as simple as clicking a button. But all the mindsets will require intentionality to be changed. As noted theologian Moo stated, "We develop the mindset of the Spirit, but only if the mind is really involved."[29] Fixed mindsets can become growth mindsets though. Isn't that good news? We detox when we examine the mindset to see what resembles the mind of Christ and what doesn't.

Since I don't see Jesus in a rush, what is it about the rush that we need to let go of? Maybe it is expectations, demands, pleasing man, or the pursuit of our own glory. Or maybe there are legitimate reasons we are hurried. Perhaps we feel passionate about what we are doing, and we are doing it for the glory of God. Even then, there might be elements of the hurried mindset we need to let go of so we can do the work of the Lord in peace.

Tip 2: Prune

Pruning seems painful. When my husband hacks down a tree, er, excuse me, prunes it, sometimes that poor shrub looks ugly. It looks like it hurt. But when the next season rolls around, what do we see? Beautiful fruit. Sometimes discerning what needs pruning is the hard part. We don't want to let go of what we know or our routine. But maybe our life needs to look different and be less hurried. Pruning behaviors can be as important as pruning activities.

Tip 3: Pause

I love this word. It reminds me to rest. Rest does not have to mean lying down. We can rest right in the middle of whatever we are doing. For me, I rest by reading or hearing Scripture. First thing in the morning, when the house is quiet, is my favorite time. Even when I am busy, if I make myself stop and abide in Jesus, it helps me to rest and rejuvenate. Pausing helps us tweak our current activity. Maybe, like Mary, as we sit in Christ's presence, we will be refreshed and able to do exceedingly more than we thought possible—just not in a hurried manner.

Tip 4: Work Smarter, Not Harder

I had not heard the term "workaholic" applied to me until the past few years. The idiom "keep one's nose to the grindstone," is vivid imagery for one who works hard. But we can find ways to make our work "work" for us.

I like to work alongside others, and I found sometimes, when I was cooking and cleaning, my children would be lying around waiting for dinner. So I started inviting them to work with me. With their help, the tasks were done more quickly, and we got in some quality time as well. This practice is especially helpful around the holidays. At big gatherings everyone in our family makes or contributes to the feast. Working smarter does not necessarily mean having to multitask. We can include others in our work, enjoying their company and strengths in the process.

Tip 5: Worship like Mary

"Mary has chosen the good portion, which will not be taken away from her" (Luke 10:42b, ESV). Worshiping God is our portion. God did not make us to worship for only one hour on Sunday morning. It is meant to be a part of our everyday life.

A good example of this truth was Daniel. Daniel placed the spiritual exercises of worshiping and praying throughout each day. "Now when Daniel learned that the decree had been published, he went home to his upstairs room where the windows opened toward Jerusalem. Three times a day he got down on his knees and prayed, giving thanks to his God, just as he had done before (Daniel 6:10, NIV). Worship is what we are created to do. It affects our mindsets and washes our mind with truth, cleansing us from the bombardment of 70,000-plus thoughts a day. When worship starts our day, it puts everything into perspective, beginning our day with the mind of Christ. Continuing our day with God-centered reminders is important as well.

Getting to the Root

More is not always better—and at times may actually be harmful. It turns out the hurried mindset can keep us in a state of overstimulation, inducing stress that can be harmful to our health and negatively affecting our personalities. It's not worth it. God created us to live for Him in relationship, not live for productivity. Christ showed us how to have a busy life but not live like it. He was not in a hurry. We can't picture Jesus running or rushing to the next ministry obligation, can we? Yet He accomplished so much.

Mindset of Christ

I have pulled some all-nighters in my day, and even some 24-hour prayer events. But Christ regularly demonstrated that his time with God was not rushed. Christ was in the center of God's will, not man's. Man would have made Christ a political hero with lots of appointments. But Jesus made sure to seek the Father for direction. "In these days he went out to the mountain to pray, and all night he continued in prayer to God" (Luke 6:12, ESV).

Jesus picked His 12 disciples after this long night of prayer. He was not in a hurried mindset or under pressure like we so often place ourselves. Christ's strength came from the Father, and Christ is our strength. We need to slow down and spend time with Him to be able to do what He has called us to do.

Mind Renewal: Keys to Unlock Our Mind

Key Thought:

"We have to slow the rhythm of rush in our lives so that the best of who we are can emerge."[30] —Lysa TerKeurst

Key Verse: Truth from God's Word

"Look carefully then how you walk, not as unwise but as wise, making the best use of the time, because the days are evil" (Ephesians 5:15-16, ESV).

Key Change: Application—Making Margin in Your Life

Spend some time in prayer and ask God to help you examine your life to see what you need to let go of and what could be shifted to a lower gear. God will give you the time you need, friend, when you give your time to Him first.

Counselor's Corner

"How long do you think it takes to get from here to your office?" my husband grinned at me.

I cast him an annoyed glance. "I know it's 22 minutes, not 17."

You see, I am a recovering time scientist. I, like many of my clients, underestimate how long it will take me to get from place to place. Because I also frequently overestimate the time it takes to complete unpleasurable tasks, I tend to dread and avoid them. Sound familiar?

A hurried lifestyle creates hurried energy and thoughts that create chemicals similar to a crisis response in our bodies. In the middle of an ultrafast pace, something unexpected will occur. When we're already living at breakneck speed, who has time for an appliance repair, an accident, bad weather, traffic, or a health issue? When we encounter typical life challenges, we panic because we feel we absolutely don't have time for them.

The truth is, we don't have time for them because we haven't blocked out time for the unexpected to occur. Instead, we've filled every waking moment—and then some—with all types of activity. When the unforeseen happens in an already overcrowded schedule, it creates a fight, flight, or freeze response that overloads our brains and bodies.

Some of us are even wired to feel guilty or believe we are bad stewards of our time if we leave huge chunks unscheduled. I'll never forget the freedom I felt when my current coach, Alli Worthington, encouraged me to block off space on my calendar during a workday to watch *Scooby Doo* with my son or schedule other "blow-off" times when I get to choose whatever I want to do in that moment. She advised that giving ourselves margin energizes us, especially when our work involves creativity.

Scheduling time blocks of freedom ushers in joy—both in the anticipation and the doing. I also need downtime to process my thoughts because a lot of my life is spent being "on" and not having much time to reflect. When I'm giving an interview or counseling a client, I'm concentrating on their thoughts and emotions and reading their body language. The personal impact I experience from secondary trauma, exposure to darkness, and absorption of clients' intense feelings cannot be ignored if I want to avoid caregiver fatigue and burnout.

Creating margin in our lives decreases our stress and anxiety levels. When we hurry, our bodies release hormones that impact our health, weight, and muscular tension in the long term. I am one of those people who, in some ways, could have lived ten lives. Friends tell me that because I have already had multiple careers, held multiple licenses, and am a recognized expert in multiple areas of mental health, God created me as a multi-passionate person. I love and find satisfaction in my chosen profession. However, I also have experienced the physical, emotional, mental, and spiritual burnout from staying highly engaged for longer periods of time than God created humans to sustain.

I once had a highly productive and energetic entrepreneurial client ask me, "What's the difference between laziness and resting?" I now use the response God gave me in that moment as my own criteria, my indicator for setting aside moments to rest. "If you are accomplishing the priorities God has called you to in regard to your parenting, personhood, marriage, and work, then you aren't lazy." My client loved the answer. It freed her up from obsessing about filling all her time and feeling guilty when she wasn't busy. This client could enjoy her downtime because she was still fulfilling God's purposes in her life—one of which is rest.

We also need to take breaks from our thoughts. Distraction, when not utilized to the point of being an unhealthy escape, is a great coping skill and an important part of dialectical behavioral therapy. I like the exercise of writing because it's a great way to slow down my thoughts since my brain can work only as fast as my pen can move or fingers can type.

Finally, practicing stillness lets us experience God more fully and rest in Him (Psalm 46:10). I like to practice stillness by focusing on my breath. Sometimes I breathe in the love of God and exhale my worries. While breathing in deeply, I say, "God, I know you want me to cast all my cares upon you because you care for me (1 Peter 5:7)." While breathing out, I say, "I don't need to worry about where my son will go to college." Lately, I've also been breathing in one nostril, holding the other closed, and out the other. Then, I repeat the practice three times, followed by breathing in and out through both. Does my mind ever wander? Absolutely. I expect it to, and when it does, I redirect my focus and begin again.

Mindset Movement 1: *Practice spiritual breathing.*

Mindset Movement 2: *Block off "do nothing" time on your calendar.*

Chapter Nine

The Lonely Mindset: Battling Grief and Isolation

> "God places the lonely in families; he sets the prisoners free and gives them joy. But he makes the rebellious live in a sun-scorched land."
>
> —Psalm 68:6, NLT

There is something about the sound of a faraway train that evokes the feeling of loneliness in me. That sound reminds me of a time when I felt so very alone. During this hard time, I felt like I had nobody in whom I could confide. My parents were divorced. Then the parent I was living with divorced again, and I had to go live with the other parent. There was an emptiness in my soul that nothing could fill.

I didn't know where I belonged, or if anyone cared. As I moved to another state, where I knew no one and navigated a tense home environment, a stepparent was introduced into the mix. There in that new place I cried myself to sleep each night, and I would hear a train whistle pierce through the dark. That sound let me know there was another reality other than the one I was living.

Seeing the Unseen

Loneliness has a way of making us feel unseen, as if we don't matter. These feelings might stem from rejection, mistreatment, or lack of self-worth. But there is a God who not only sees us, but He understands the lonely soul because He was one, too. In Psalm 68:6 shown above, the word for lonely is the Hebrew word *yâchîyd*. It occurs six times in the Old Testament, translated as "only," "only begotten son," "beloved," and "solitary."[31] When David wrote this, the loneliness he encountered hiding out in caves fleeing from Saul was not too distant of a memory. David was acquainted with extreme loneliness and knew what it was to be ostracized, threatened, and rejected.

This word is equivalent to the Greek word *yhios*, which occurs 382 times in the New Testament and is also used to refer to Jesus, the only begotten son of God.[32] Jesus came in loneliness to save many. Isaiah prophesied of the suffering from loneliness and grief that Jesus encountered. "He was despised and abandoned by men, a man of great pain and familiar with sickness; and like one from whom people hide their faces, He was despised, and we had no regard for Him" (Isaiah 53:3, NASB). The ESV says Jesus was "a man of sorrows and acquainted with grief."

Why would Jesus, who was God, choose to come in such a manner? As we keep reading in Isaiah, we find out: "However, it was our sicknesses that He Himself bore, and our pains that He carried; yet we ourselves assumed that He had been afflicted, struck down by God, and humiliated" (Isaiah 53:4, NASB). Friends, Christ bore our loneliness, our pain, our suffering, and our grief. He bore it all. What does this mean, and how do we apply this truth?

Primarily we know Jesus understands. He has compassion on us. We will still walk through suffering in this life, but we can look to Jesus in that suffering. Focusing on our suffering keeps us isolated. David wrote of the freedom God has for those imprisoned in loneliness and the subsequent joy God brings to them. Will we accept this gift? We have been set free and can have joy no matter the circumstances around us, just like Jesus did.

Provision for the Lonely

The lonely are not forgotten. God takes special care of them. But sometimes we will need to let go of our expectations. In the wreckage of our lives when we find ourselves alone, we can try to rebuild on our own, to put things back in place the way we think they should be. But God has something better in mind.

Loneliness can be provoked by our clinging to the past or to an ideal that no longer exists. The former paradigm of living for this life will set us up to fail every time. Our loneliness stems from looking for life from things that cannot give life. They can bring joy for a while, but eternal joy comes only from Jesus.

When I navigated through life as a single parent, it was a very lonely time for me. The pain inside my soul from the grief of our situation and the feelings of isolation were at times too much to bear. No one else understood. But Jesus did. Not only did He understand, but He went through loneliness and great suffering to get to me. He's done the same for every one of us. What kind of love is this? It is hard to explain, but there amid the most pain of my life, I had an inner joy as I considered how much my God loved me to show His love like that. The realization of God's love for me took the sting out of the loneliness. My soul began to miss Heaven more than the things of this earth.

God has a way of placing the lonely in families, and families can look different than a traditional grouping of only parents and their biological children. Families can look like neighbors who help one another get through a tough season. Families may form from a church small group that fills in the gap for each other. And like in the book of Ruth, a family may emerge from a kinsman redeemer God puts directly on our path. But always, Jesus fills the emptiness of our souls that nothing else can fill.

As I struggled to parent my five children through a harrowing five-year-long court battle in the wake of the revelation of their father's sin, God had something in mind for me. I wasn't forgotten. Neither was my husband-to-be who also had been parenting on his own. And now my "Bo" (short for Boaz) and I are happily wed and are witnesses to the truth that the lonely are remembered. God takes care of us.

However, I must add a disclaimer here: Redemption is messy. Christ bled to redeem us. The fusing together of lives is a messy miracle. It takes time for wounds to heal. It isn't perfect. And when God does not bring along a kinsman redeemer, friends, He wants to be the husband to us. Whatever situation evokes loneliness in our soul, God sees us—always. We are never forgotten. We can trust God's provision for us; He was a lonely soul, too.

A Word About Grief

When we think about suffering, it's hard not to think about Job. In his suffering, Job's friends brought him no relief. Job told them so: "Your memorable sayings are proverbs of ashes, your defenses are defenses of clay" (Job 13:12, NASB). Pat answers and clichéd sayings cannot heal the soul overcome with grief. No words can comfort the grief stricken; only the hope we have in Christ can. When we seek to help others encumbered with grief—or perhaps even help ourselves—the most important truth to remember is Christ has not left us alone.

No one else experiences an identical suffering. So in this way, like loneliness, grief isolates us. As Solomon pointed out, "The heart knows its own bitterness, and no stranger shares its joy" (Proverbs 14:10, ESV). People don't need polite sayings when their world is falling apart. They need Jesus. They need to understand the here and now in light of eternity to make sense of the nonsensical. For it is when we see our suffering in comparison with Christ's that we understand all are destined to suffer in this fallen world. And Christ has paved the way for us.

Fear of death is one of our most challenging concerns. It is final, after all. However, even though Christ took the sting out of death, we can still think this life is all there is and live in fear of death. We grieve at the reality that we are finite, but Christ offers us eternity. We grieve because we want this life to be our hope, but thank God, it isn't. God invites us in our grief to lay aside our former hope and pick up His.

There is a secret place in Christ that is our comfort in those moments when the pain and grief are too much to bear. There we can say with Job, "Though He slay me, I will hope in Him" (Job 13:15a, NASB). Job knew if he could just talk with God, he would find his cure. This is what the grief-stricken soul needs. Christ alone. God is good, friend, even in our grief. None of our suffering will be wasted, and He wants to be our comfort.

The Danger of Isolation

One of the core strategies most often employed during grief is isolation. The enemy seeks to isolate us. If he can separate us from God in our mind, he can try to pick us off. In our minds the evil one blames God as the cause of our grief. But this is not true, nor does it soothe our pain. And in our isolation, our pain only deepens.

Isolation can also cause us to sin. "Whoever isolates himself seeks his own desire; he breaks out against all sound judgment." (Proverbs 18:1, ESV). Isolation is different than solitude. With isolation, we can give ourselves over to being self-focused as we commiserate on our loneliness or grief. In such a place, the enemy works. We don't think properly when we give in to our thoughts of grief or isolation. In contrast, solitude can be a source of life when we focus our thoughts on God's Word. "My son, do not let wisdom and understanding out of your sight, preserve sound judgment and discretion" (Proverbs 3:21, NIV).

A Lesson from the Shunamite Woman

Emotions are also the catalyst of whether we process grief in a healthy way or stay stagnant in our sorrow. The way out of grief is not by trying to go around it. Emotions do not have to control us. They can be the very tool that helps us get victory as we cry out to God.

Tucked in the book of 2 Kings is a little story about a Shunamite woman that has taught me much about overcoming grief. This woman finally got the son she had yearned and waited for, then tragedy struck:

> "And the child grew. Now it happened one day that he went out to his father, to the reapers. And he said to his father, 'My head, my head!' So he said to a servant, 'Carry him to his mother.' When he had taken him and brought him to his mother, he sat on her knees till noon, and then died. And she went up and laid him on the bed of the man of God, shut the door upon him, and went out. Then she called to her husband, and said, 'Please send me one of the young men and one of the donkeys, that I may run to the man of God and come back.' So he said, 'Why are you going to him today? It is neither the New Moon nor the Sabbath.' And she said, 'It is well.' Then she saddled a donkey, and said to her servant, 'Drive, and go forward; do not slacken the pace for me unless I tell you.' And so she departed, and went to the man of God at Mount Carmel" (2 King 4:18-25, NKJV).

What was the woman's response? It blows me away. The Shunamite woman did not give in to the grief. She knew she had to act quickly. She wasn't going to accept this loss sitting down. Sometimes in the shock of our loss, we are upheld by the mighty arms of God while we try to process our new reality. This woman held onto her faith in God as she made her way to Elisha. And when Elisha asked how she was, she again answered, "It is well." Then she lost it.

It's OK to not be OK. She was not in denial when she said, "It is well." The woman was moving in faith. Then she needed to grieve. "Now when she came to the man of God at the hill, she caught him by the feet, but Gehazi came near to push her away. But the man of God said, 'Let her alone; for her soul is in deep distress, and the LORD has hidden it from me, and has not told me'" (2 Kings 4:27, NKJV).

The story ended well for the Shunamite woman. God healed her precious son. But what happens when we don't like our story and are stuck in grief? God meets us in that place and tells us it is well as we place our trust in Him.

The Source of Loneliness

Loneliness is not just being alone. It is a loneliness of soul that can be felt in a crowded room; it's an awareness of self that is on steroids. Loneliness comes from our mindset, not from those around us. Ironically, these days we are more in contact with others than ever before through social media, yet we are also quite possibly the most isolated we have ever been. We can be in a room full of people and still not know community.

Our mindset determines whether we feel isolated or welcomed. Many triggers lead to loneliness: going through personal trials and sorrows, struggling for acceptance with different personalities or social groups, facing rejection. However, our loneliness of soul and grief-stricken hearts can be healed as our perspective changes, and we learn how to approach grief and isolation with Christ and others.

Trigger 1: Emotions

When our mind lies to us, telling us no one cares, we must do battle. Simply surrounding ourselves with others will not bring us lasting peace from the lonesome mindset. Only the One who designed us can do that. "Peace I leave with you; my peace I give to you. Not as the world gives do I give to you. Let not your hearts be troubled, neither let them be afraid" (John 14:27, ESV). People let us down. They cannot comfort us like Jesus can. Jesus Himself did not trust man. "But Jesus on his part did not entrust himself to them, because he knew all people" (John 2:24, ESV). When we put our emotions in control of our belief system, we can become deceived and led by feelings rather than reality.

Conversations with my kids over the years have shown just how much loneliness can be provoked by our own emotions, often fanned into flame by presumptions. We think no one wants to be around us, or we assume certain people don't like us. Imagination can get the better of us. It is wiser not to listen to our emotions without first examining our circumstance through Scripture to keep our mindset in line.

Trigger 2: Connection

Today we are so connected yet disconnected. Social media is a form of connection, but it's certainly not equal to meeting face-to-face. At the time of writing this, a pandemic is making connection so very hard. We are all wearing masks and fearing to touch one another, which has disturbed our sense of connection at church, in families, and in our culture. But we can still find connection.

Joining a small group is critical to our faith. We may need to search to find a group that fits but having such a community to belong to is crucial to building up our spirits and to healing a lonely mindset. Connection with others keeps our burdens from overwhelming us.

Ultimately, we are all connected by suffering. We have no inkling of the suffering of another soul until we ourselves have suffered. Putting ourselves into close community helps lift our souls out of the chasm of grief and loneliness.

Trigger 3: Significance

A lonely mindset can emanate from our need to be validated by others. Searching for significance from a broken world, as well as searching for validation from achievements, is futile. We can feel left out or less than when we compare our situation to others' and feel ourselves to be less significant. This is the equivalent of trying to find our identity in the creation rather than in God. Adopting the mindset of a child of God, we can choose to let go of the pursuit for significance from things that cannot provide our worth. Finding our worth in the creation rather than in the Creator will leave us on empty.

Trigger 4: Despair

Life can bring us many pains and sorrows, but God can deliver us through them all. When we are given to despair, we have an ever-present help that is real. Such challenges to our faith reveal where our help truly comes from. The choice is up to us.

Trying to escape grief by running to anything other than God for relief just won't satisfy. In fact, doing so might actually intensify our pain. God did not promise to remove our problems, but He did promise that His grace is enough for any problem we face. We just have to ask. "When the righteous cry for help, the LORD hears and delivers them out of all their troubles. The LORD is near to the brokenhearted and saves the crushed in spirit. Many are the afflictions of the righteous, but the LORD delivers him out of them all" (Psalm 34:17-19, ESV).

Trigger 5: Isolation

Isolation hinders healing. We were meant to live in community, and God uses others to speak into our lives. Loneliness has a cure. Fellowship with God's people is a part of God's plan. When the circle we are in does not help us heal, we might need to find ourselves a healthier community. God did not want Adam to be alone, and He does not want any of the rest of us to be alone either.

We Are Not Alone

Sometimes we can get so absorbed in our loneliness we forget we are not alone. This is not just a religious phrase; it is a promise and a reality. Living into that reality and being aware of the presence of God are what make His presence tangible. When we feel lonely, we can cry out to God like the psalmist did: "Turn to me and be gracious to me, for I am lonely and afflicted" (Psalm 25:16, ESV).

The word for lonely here is the same word found in Psalm 68, "Here *yāḥîd* means 'solitary,' 'isolated,' 'lonely.'"[33] God cares about the lonely. The loneliness of the soul is healed when we draw near to God. "Praise the Lord; praise God our savior! For each day he carries us in his arms" (Psalm 68:19, NLT). We don't have to carry the loneliness with us anymore. God is with us.

Tip 1: Pray for Godly Friends

When my children felt lonely or isolated, I asked them if they asked God for friends. The mindset of loneliness is often our fault. We can feel bummed because people don't seek us out, but do we seek them? Sometimes we just need to pray, plan a little, pump up our courage, and reach out. When a friendship does not work out, we can ask God to help us find our tribe.

Tip 2: Acceptance

We can feel isolated when we don't accept our lot. Our struggle to move forward can be severely hindered by the lonely mindset, which holds us back with shame as we focus on other people's rejection of us. To many of us, suffering feels embarrassing. The presence of suffering in our lives is isolating in and of itself until we accept our circumstances as being allowed from God.

For example, in the middle of the pandemic I was diagnosed with melanoma, which was incredibly hard. The pain of the skin removal procedure and my adjustment to the chunk of my head and hair that was removed are still things I honestly grieve when I touch that part of my scalp. But I let myself grieve. Now I choose to accept this is part of my story where God can receive all the glory.

Instead of focusing on the pain God brought me through, I marvel that the melanoma was only 1 millimeter away from advancing to the next stage of cancer. We must let go of what we know in order to leave the lonely mindset. The same God who was with us before will also be there for us in our new normal. The biblical character of Job is a great example of this truth.

Tip 3: Make Time for Who Is Important

Life's busyness can keep us bound in loneliness or grief. (Chapter Eight: "The Hurried Mindset" provides help about how to exit that thought framework.) To fight this, we can schedule recurring times with those who matter most to us. When we build these people into our life, our isolation will decrease. These days this is as simple as entering a name in a reminder or calendar app, so we don't forget to make time for our most important relationships.

Tip 4: Positioning Ourselves

As most of my children have grown up and moved into new situations, invariably the lonely ache in their souls rises to the point where they share it with me. God made us for fellowship. It is so important, though, that we seek out godly community to build us up in Christ.

Each time my children have experienced this loneliness, I asked them to consider their position. I encouraged them to position themselves to be in a place of God's blessing and where they could meet people by joining a good church or a small group study with people their age. Each time they did, it wasn't long until I received a call about the new people they met. We don't have to defeat loneliness on our own. We must position ourselves near others because we were made for community.

Tip 5: Embracing Solitude

Although God created us to be people in community with one another, we also need times when we go off by ourselves and spend time with Jesus. Jesus modeled this for us. At times my kids have said they can't stand being alone in social environments. It was embarrassing to them. If we are not careful, we can feel as if our worth is found in others. In contrast, solitude often feels like a sweet refuge.

When it is just God and us, we are aware of ourselves apart from all else. Finding moments of solitude is super hard for young moms. As a mother of five, I know. But as paradoxical as it sounds, solitude is part of the cure to loneliness. During such times we are OK by ourselves, especially as we take time to meditate on God's Word and talk with Jesus. In our solitude we discover afresh who we are apart from anyone else's definition. Being alone does not have to be lonely. It can be a refreshing reminder of who we are in Christ. With Him, we are never alone.

Getting to the Root

Gripped with grief, we can be afraid to hope for any relief and can be tempted to go to the wrong place for comfort. Busying or numbing ourselves will not heal our lonely souls. Our sorrows often lead us to isolation, where we suffer silently and accept our sentence of loneliness. However, we can break free when we recognize the path we are on and cry out to God for help. God alone can heal the wounds of the soul. The mindset of despair can become a mindset of hope when our hope is fixed in the right place: above circumstances and in the eternal Christ alone.

Mindset of Christ

Christ did not pursue popularity to fill His place of need with others. "But he would withdraw to desolate places and pray" (Luke 5:16, ESV). Only God can fill the empty place in our soul. Throngs of people surrounded Jesus, but this was not something He needed. He filled His need for community with the Father and those closest to Him.

When we let God fill us and make us whole, we can then come into community with others and have something with which to offer and encourage them. As Paul stated, "Well, my brothers and sisters, let's summarize. When you meet together, one will sing, another will teach, another will tell some special revelation God has given, one will speak in tongues, and another will interpret what is said. But everything that is done must strengthen all of you" (1 Corinthians 14:26, NLT).

Mind Renewal: Keys to Unlock Our Mind

Key Thought: Loneliness is a state of mind.

Key Verse: Truth from God's Word

"He heals the brokenhearted and binds up their wounds" (Psalm 147:3, NIV).

Key Change: Application—Releasing Grief and Embracing Acceptance in Christ

It's OK to let go of grief. We don't have to own it or be loyal to it. We are not defined by what we go through. Write down what you need to let go of, so it no longer has a hold of you. This can be in your journal or on a piece of paper that you rip up or set ablaze.

Counselor's Corner

We were created for connection. This is easy to say, but for many of us living high-demand lives, planning time with others seems an almost insurmountable task. Women struggling with low support must overcome three obstacles to create community: having confidence that someone would want to spend time with us; making time with friends a priority (even when we don't feel like it); and being willing to cast a wide net of invites to get girl time on the calendar.

Attaching to others begins when we are babies and develops over the relationships we experience in our lifetime. When we grow up knowing someone is there to catch us and we are loved unconditionally, we relax when we connect with others. Unfortunately, all of us have experienced moments of rejection and betrayal. If these moments reoccur too often, our tolerance for risk decreases, which can lead to social anxiety. This anxiety can manifest itself in unconscious relationship sabotage or intimacy avoidance.

We are all worthy of being loved, not only by a God who loves us but also by others who have learned through Him to love well. If you struggle with believing you are God's gift to our world, you will want to rehearse Scriptures like Psalm 139:14, which affirms you are "wonderfully made" so your confidence will grow. Maybe your awareness of your weaknesses makes you feel like no one will like you. You might have even been told by an adult in your childhood there was something wrong with you and that was a reason why you didn't have many friends. For example, as a natural talker, a weakness of mine is listening well and not interrupting. The best place for me to practice my listening skills is not alone but with others. You may struggle with an opposite issue. You may need to work on talking more so people can get to know you better.

We can't change our relational weaknesses or experience positive connection in solitude. Learning to securely attach involves being with and interacting with others. Recently, I had a client who had to take a huge leap of faith even to be vulnerable with me, her counselor. She fought the belief that if people truly knew her, they wouldn't see her value, would only see her shortcomings, and would reject her. When I still admired her as the amazing leader she is after she allowed me to see her flaws, insecurities, and struggles, this allowed her to experience secure attachment in a safe space. This client is now tentatively taking the next step. Whether in a structured group or one-on-one with a few women, she is opening her heart and life up to others so she can experience their embrace as well. What if they don't? I'll be there to remind her that's their problem not hers, and she can try again with someone else.

Trying to build relationships without any guarantees takes guts, but the reward of long-term mutually supportive relationships is worth the risk. To win at this game, we have to play often and with more than one option. For example, I recently wanted to have a small celebration with my closest friends. I made a list of nine people to invite. A few had immediate conflicts, leaving me with the five that comfortably fit in the restaurant space. Before the day of the event, two more needed to cancel due to work, exhaustion, and health issues. I didn't let the cancellations get me down but instead had the best time with the three friends who came, and in the end, it felt like the perfect number. When I have a free night and want to go out or have someone over, I often call or text half a dozen friends before I find a "yes." Some of these friends I know better than others, but with every encounter, we build deeper relationships filled with mutual sharing, lamenting, and laughter.

Mindset Movement: *Make a list of at least ten people you'd like to get to know better. Choose a couple of different time options when you can do something with at least one of them, and then start inviting until you find one whose schedule syncs with yours. If you feel a lot of insecurity with this assignment, prepare ahead of time, and write a response you will say if they can't commit and words of reassurance you can say to yourself while completing this task.*

Chapter Ten

The Scarcity Mindset—Battling Covetousness and Lust

"My flesh and my heart may fail, but God is the strength of my heart and my portion forever."

—Psalm 73:26, ESV

"I'm on a diet, y'all," I said. "Please don't bring junk in the house or offer me any."

Groans filled the air.

"Not again."

"You can do it, Mom," my son added. "Don't give up this time."

Ugh. Now that the word was on the street, the constant accountability would come. There is nothing as irritating as having family members question one's food choices.

"Mom, what are you eating? Is that allowed on your diet?"

I could understand if I were eating a Whopper and fries, but why did they have to hound me about the little things? But as soon as that thought came to my mind, a more helpful thought surfaced. I began to realize it was the little things that added up and caused me to stumble.

People in general don't want to be "deprived" or have less than what they've grown accustomed to. Whether it is belongings, relationships, finances, or food, a scarcity mindset is born when we think we don't have our fair share. The biggest example in my life is food. As I have grown older, my body does not require as much food as it used to, and so the reality of being on a perpetual fast of sorts does not bode well for this sister.

It Happens by Degrees

Each time I start a new weight-loss endeavor, my mind is fixed on my goal. This last time I even had a friend join me in setting goals, and I made a chart. I was serious. But the scent of baked goods usually weakens my resolve. I'm a sucker for that smell. Kids show up, and I bake and test goodies. As I contemplate why my children can eat what I can't, the scarcity mentality sets in. A scarcity mindset makes us feel deprived, like we don't get what we deserve. It reflects on what we can't have rather than what we do have. The comparison trap weaves its way around our hearts and can turn our craving into coveting as we are dissatisfied with God's provision.

My particular stumbling blocks are the skinny people who can eat whatever and how much they want and still be a size 2. This is where coveting comes in. I wish I had a different metabolism. But the cravings are my real problem. Am I the only one who has started a diet at 7 a.m. and ignores it by 11 a.m.? I have had a tendency to indulge my yearnings, and it takes me off the path of healthy eating by degrees or leaps.

After many failed diet attempts, I finally realized my strategy was akin to the definition of insanity—doing the same thing over and over again and expecting different results. What could I do? Get back up and figure out how I got outsmarted—again. But instead of a weakening resolve that throws in the towel, I began to study the reasons I made bad choices. Behind my weight-loss battle was a scarcity mindset maybe we all can relate to. We might not like to own our struggle, but until we name what we're thinking and feeling, we can't move forward victoriously. A scarcity mindset revolves around covetousness and lust that longs for more than its share. In the last few years my scarcity mindset has involved food; I don't want to let go of anything less than "my" portion.

Mindset Overhaul

I needed a mindset change that was about more than food and weight loss. For so long I said I just wanted to be healthy and didn't care about the pounds. However, the truth is I just wanted to look good (a touch of pride there, I know). That kind of weight loss does not change hearts and minds. The same behavior can pop up again and again if I don't change my mind about how I view food intake and my physical appearance. After all, if what God was showing me about mindsets was true—that we have the power to overcome our negative thoughts through Christ—then I should see real results, results that are not just about transforming my external habits but my internal desires, too.

Like the helpless mindset, I found the chief triggers for the scarcity mindset all center around the word "enough." When we don't feel like we have enough of what we want or need, we live in the mindset of lack. In the area of food, we can buy into the definition of "enough" as prescribed by our culture. One meal at a fast-food joint is an entire day's worth of calories. Is that enough? Or way too much? When we grow accustomed to those portion sizes, the reality of what we truly need gets distorted. We can forget to listen to what we truly need and chase after what we really don't. God wants to satisfy the pain point in our lives that feels it can't find satisfaction. He can do that. God is enough. He helps direct our food portions and anything else we bring into our minds. But we must lay down our idols first.

Victory Starts by Not Being a Victim

Through many failed diets and then revelations as I studied God's Word, I have begun to let go of the portion I thought I deserved. I had to recognize I am not a victim. Needing less is actually a blessing. Wanting more than I need is gluttony. It is hard to write that word, but it is true. I had to bring my scarcity mindset under a biblical perspective and understand how my desires line up with God's desires. I needed God's Word to overcome my mindset.

Lack of self-control also contributes to a scarcity mindset. Asking for accountability helps when we are weak. One way of doing this is splitting a meal with my husband when we eat out. Sometimes half a restaurant serving feels like too much. The scarcity mentality is enabled by a lavish sense that says to us, "We deserve a treat or dessert." But now I have sugar-free versions of favorites, or I grab a piece of fruit or a veggie while my family eats the "normal" food. Accepting a new norm helps us to let go of our former normal, which probably should not have been normal after all.

Friend, I have not arrived. But God has revealed this weakness in me, and I am no longer a slave to it. And I am finally seeing real progress. I may never be back down to a size 5 but striving after a certain dress size can also be idolatry. What means more to me now is gratitude for my portion. Wanting more than my portion no longer has a hold on me. I continue to be aware of triggers that propel me into a scarcity mindset, but now I have strategies to overcome them. Perhaps you can relate to some of the areas listed below where the scarcity mentality thrives and find tools and victory in overcoming the scarcity mindset in all of life.

Scarcity Mindset: Famine

A lack of food is famine. Where I live, we have so much food available that we are not truly acquainted with this concept. On a vision trip to Guatemala with Compassion International, I met people who lived in the shadow of famine and yet were generous with what they had, providing hospitality to us. That trip changed me. My historic struggle to want more when I had more than enough came from a surprising place. Somewhere in that desire for more was a fear that I would be hungry. I had a different famine in my mind, and food could not satisfy that place—only God could. Could I give my desires for a bigger or better provision to God? Could He be my portion instead of the things my heart chased after? Could I say with Jeremiah that my hope was in Him, not in my portion? "'The Lord is my portion,' says my soul, 'therefore I will hope in him'" (Lamentations 3:24, ESV). Yes, I could. But changing my mindset took time.

My portion had to stop being fueled by entitlement or comparison and instead be calibrated to what I truly needed, not what I wanted. What felt like famine was actually freedom. I had been programmed to believe a larger portion size is the norm. Many restaurants have a portion size that is gargantuan. Commercials tell us we will have joy if we indulge ourselves with as much food as we want. Mindsets are not formed overnight, and it takes doses of truth over time to reset our mindset. Though I still fail at times, God has shown me He can satisfy me more than a meal ever could. Former habits can be replaced with new ones to reorient our mindset:

- Now I delight to give the bigger portion to others. Splitting meals or just getting an appetizer minimizes portion size.
- When I switch gears and focus on worshipping God, thanking Him for who He is, I'm looking to Him rather than food to fill me.
- Filling my mind with His Word not only takes away the lack in my mindset, but it centers me where I need to be, coming back to Him for my needs.
- Removing myself from tempting situations and reminding myself of biblical principles keeps me from a scarcity mindset.
- Praying for God to fill in the areas where I feel like I'm not enough or don't have enough keeps my focus on Him, not me.

God knows our needs and promises to provide for them, but not necessarily for all our wants. His provision is perfect. "And God is able to bless you abundantly, so that in all things at all times, having all that you need, you will abound in every good work" (2 Corinthians 9:8, NIV).

Scarcity Mindset: Competitive Spirit

A competitive spirit is also an indicator we are striving for more. Competition is sparked by an innate desire to be the best, ultimately to have what we want. We see this in various pursuits: raising our children, our job, our home, and other tangibles. Scrambling for position or provision comes from doubting God will provide "the best" for us, so we need to grab it for ourselves. If we step in and make things happen, we don't have to rely on or wait for God. Is this mindset familiar? However, as Glynnis Whitwer put it so well, when we worry if there is enough pie to go around, God just makes a bigger pie.[34] There is enough to go around, friend. God's provision and position for us is tailored just for us, no one else.

The problem is many of us don't believe God can or will provide for us, but God knows our needs. "The young lions suffer want and hunger; but those who seek the LORD lack no good thing" (Psalm 34:10, ESV). Why do we have trouble trusting this verse? Maybe it's because the way God provides is not the way we think He should. We have goals, and we want them satisfied. When those doors don't open for us, we can feel forgotten. But those who seek the Lord will lack no good thing.

We don't truly lack when we are in the Lord. We just need to trust that God's will is best. His provision in our lives is not about us but about Him. He gives us what we need not so we can point to ourselves as successes, but so we can point others to our great Provider and the One behind every victory.

The scarcity mindset led by a competitive spirit never has enough applause or attention, and there's always another new thing to be desired coming down the production line. This is idolatry, as well. The scarcity mindset is fueled by comparison. Comparing to others robs us of contentment and joy in God's specific plan for us. Where God guides, God provides.

Scarcity Mindset: Relationships

Most of us grow up believing we will marry well; we will marry someone who will fulfill and complete us. When this is not our reality, we feel the pain as we see others enjoying relationships we thought we would have. God's plans are different for everyone.

If we are not careful, we can allow a scarcity mentality to drive us to fill our lack on our own. Sometimes in our pursuit of a relationship, we end up in a relationship outside of God's will. "Don't team up with those who are unbelievers. How can righteousness be a partner with wickedness? How can light live with darkness?" (2 Corinthians 6:14, NLT). Having a right relationship with God first helps us to be ready for other relationships without making them an idol.

Scarcity Mindset: Finances

My husband lost three jobs in five years due to government contracts falling through. That season taught us lessons we will never forget. Each time we encountered a new job loss, we adjusted our spending. We prayed, we trusted, and we drew nearer to God.

But beneath our courage were challenges that threatened to overtake our faith. Bills continued to come. Feeding five hungry mouths was a grim reality. The government medical plan did not cover adults—including the asthma medication I needed. When we were tempted to give in to a scarcity mindset, we overcame it by focusing on God's promises.

During times when we could have been tempted to think our portion was not enough, God's purpose was to teach us to be content in whatever provision we had. As Paul said in Philippians, "… I have learned to be content whatever the circumstances. I know what it is to be in need, and I know what it is to have plenty. I have learned the secret of being content in any and every situation, whether well fed or hungry, whether living in plenty or in want. I can do all this through him who gives me strength" (Philippians 4:11-13, NIV). A season of less became a season of fullness. We planted a garden that God made bloom, and we even shared the bounty with others. Miraculous provision drew us closer to God and brought Him glory. The secret was Jesus. He is our strength. When we feel tempted to cave to a scarcity mentality, He is ready to meet us and provide far above what we could ever imagine.

A Lesson from Moses

After Moses led God's people away from slavery and into the desert toward the Promised Land, the Israelites discovered a new hobby: grumbling. They craved the foods they had in Egypt. They wanted it yesterday. God was providing for them. Every day God's people could walk outside and gather manna—literally food from Heaven. They were to gather just what they needed for the day. If they gathered too much, like for the next day, it would turn into maggots. But God's children did not like having "just enough." They did not like what was being provided, how much was being provided, nor how it was being provided. I can so relate, especially after years of cooking for my own children. I empathize with God when I fix dinner for my family and wait for the praises to roll in, but instead I get complaints. However, God's children were complaining against God Almighty. They went so far as to say they would have rather *died* than have what God provided them. Woah. That became a self-fulfilling prophecy for many of them. Then they said the food they were provided when they were slaves was better. Wow.

> "And the whole congregation of the people of Israel grumbled against Moses and Aaron in the wilderness, and the people of Israel said to them, 'Would that we had died by the hand of the LORD in the land of Egypt, when we sat by the meat pots and ate bread to the full, for you have brought us out into this wilderness to kill this whole assembly with hunger'" (Exodus 16:2-3, ESV).

The Israelites' lust and idolatry bound their hearts. When the Israelites said God's intention was to kill them, they had shifted far away from just a scarcity mindset. They mingled in the victim mindset, too. The lies we believe about our portion can jade our hearts as well. God's intention is always good. The Israelites allowed their mindset to get out of hand when they believed God would seek to harm them. Is it the same with us? In my struggle, I can either complain I have to eat healthfully, or I can understand that taking care of my body prevents illness and health problems. We invite consequences when we don't walk in wisdom. We might not think we would behave like the Israelites did, but we probably have triggers of our own that plunge us into a scarcity mindset.

Trigger 1: Portion.

How much is enough? I have to admit something: My "enough" is usually not about my satisfaction. It's typically about wanting somebody else's portion. When others can have what I can't, and their portions are bigger than mine, that's when I become dissatisfied. I hate to admit this, but I used to fix the plates for dinner and eyeball the portion that looked like the most, or the best, and put it at my place. This scarcity mentality was not about lack at all. It was about desire.

Trigger 2: Provision

Behind the emotions of what we want is fear. Will God provide? Let's be honest, provision is really about wanting the most or the best according to us, not God. God has enough to go around. The righteous are not seen lacking for bread. As it says in Psalms, "I was young and now I am old, yet I have never seen the righteous forsaken or their children begging bread" (Psalm 37:25, NIV). Sometimes our belief system is fixated on what we can bring to the table. But anything we have was given to us. God is able, more than able to provide for us from His endless riches. "And my God will supply every need of yours according to his riches in glory in Christ Jesus" (Philippians 4:19, ESV). The question is, will we be content with that provision?

Trigger 3: Promises

We can also make an idol of what we think our portion or provision should be, as if everything we desire is promised to us. When that promise is seemingly broken, we slip into a scarcity mindset, looking for fulfillment from the promise rather than the Promise Maker and Keeper. God's promises are yes and amen when they are centered on kingdom purposes. But man's promises are often centered on our satisfaction, not God's glory. Sometimes the scarcity mentality can also slip into our relationships or other things we thought we were promised.

Trigger 4: Purpose

The scarcity mindset becomes entrenched in our souls when we forget the purpose behind God's provision in our lives: relationship. We don't have to hoard or worry about our portion or position. God wants us to trust Him to provide as we walk in relationship with Him. The survival instinct that kicks in the moment we think we are deprived can be changed. But we must reorient our thinking. Sometimes our feelings of lack come from another place or time in our lives. Fear hides behind our struggle with scarcity.

A New Heart

We gain victory when our mindset is transformed from one of discontentment about our lot, to one of satisfaction. Fixing ourselves on the mind of Christ brings us from want to contentment. It takes intentionality and strategies to help us move away from our triggers to self-control. Here are a few tips to help us gain the upper hand when a sense of lack is driving our mind.

Tip 1: The Practice of Contentment

The emotional part of my struggle with my diet involved food boundaries. Contentment was not going to happen because of an external measure like a diet or supportive family and friends. Changing my diet required a mindset change. Contentment is a choice made through Christ. Christ yielded and set His will on God's. "Yet I want Your will to be done, not mine" (Luke 22:42b, NLT). When faced with hunger in the desert, Christ fed on the Word of God and defeated temptation with the Word of God. We practice contentment when we recognize and expose the triggers and go to God's Word to fill us. Choosing to eat according to my desire rather than my need is greed. When we practice contentment by not wanting something out of the boundaries for us, we choose self-discipline, which guides us to freedom. "But godliness with contentment is great gain. For we brought nothing into the world, and we can take nothing out of it" (1 Timothy 6:6-7, NIV).

Tip 2: Not Mine!

Sometimes we covet because deep inside we feel looked over. We want to make sure we get our fair share. The instability of multiple divorces during my childhood created a hunger within me to be comforted. I felt invisible and insecure about my needs being met, which created within me a striving to make sure I got my fair share. If no one was going to take care of me the way I thought I should be, then I would do it myself. We seek to make something of ourselves, but Christ emptied Himself on our behalf by "taking the form of a servant, being born in the likeness of men" (Philippians 2:7b, ESV). Taking the mindset off self, we can surrender the rights we think we have, realizing God owns it all. It's not mine. Or yours. God will provide for us, and He never overlooks anyone. When we pursue God before other things, He will bless us and provide what we need.

Tip 3: A New Craving

The Israelites craved the food they ate when they were enslaved. I am pretty sure the meat they remembered and wanted was mostly gristle, but cravings are real. Surely, they would not want to be enslaved again, would they? What about that meat was so special? We can be like the Israelites and stay in a cycle of wanting, craving what is out of bounds. Or we can form a new craving for what God provides. Our new craving will require adapting to what we have and not demanding what we don't. Solomon helped me see a little dessert is permissible, but not too much: "Do you like honey? Don't eat too much, or it will make you sick!" (Proverbs 25:16, NLT). When I offer my cravings to God and choose to accept what He allows and provides, those cravings lose their power to affect my behavior. I am satisfied. Craving things never satisfies, but craving God sets me free from what I idolized. If we persevere, God changes our hearts and gives us a new desire—Him.

Tip 4 Bless Others

When we are tempted to compare ourselves to others or complain about what we have, we can resist that temptation by doing the opposite. When we succumb to the desire to bless ourselves, we end up being discontent. We never have enough. But when we seek to take what is ours and give it to someone else, we are doubly blessed. Joy and satisfaction overflow as we do what pleases the Lord. When we are faithful with a little, God will make us faithful with much. The scarcity mentality affects more than just us. When we can keep our body and attitude in check, the flesh does not control us and we can be used by God to help others.

Getting to the Root

When we struggle with a scarcity mindset, we are in essence saying we don't trust God to see and meet our needs. The mindset of scarcity can become a mindset of gratitude as we fix our eyes on Jesus and not on our lack.

Mindset of Christ

Christ did not seek His way. He accepted His humble circumstances and submitted to the Lordship of God. "But I am doing just what the Father commanded me, so that the world may know that I love the Father." (John 14:31, NET). The scarcity mindset is fixed on self and its wants. As Jesus faced temptations and attacks on His mindset, He resisted the enemy with God's Word and chose God's commands over the flesh. Friends, we must tell our flesh it is not the boss of us. God's grace can help us, but it will be a fight. When we go to God's Word to counter the negative mindsets, we rise above mindset traps not just by saying no, but by understanding the lies behind mindsets so we can be free.

Mind Renewal: Keys to Unlock Our Mind

Key Thought: Bless others when you feel lack.

Key Verse:

"But I discipline my body and keep it under control, lest after preaching to others I myself should be disqualified" (1 Corinthians 9:27, ESV).

Keys Change: Application—Facing the Battle of the Mind

The scarcity mindset can become an abundance mentality depending on our focus. Do we focus on lack or on contentment with God's provision? The One who provided for the Israelites is also the One who took five loaves and two fish and ended up with 12 baskets leftover from one boy's lunch. He can take what we have and satisfy us. Journal about what you lack, and hunt for Scriptures to reveal the truth of the scarcity mindset. Pray and write down the abundance you will reap by accepting God's portion for you.

Counselor's Corner

How do we practice abundant thinking in our lives? We begin by aligning our worldview with God's. We realize we will never experience the true abundance God has for us here on earth (1 Corinthians 2:9), and we frequently remind ourselves that we are strangers on this earth (Hebrews 11:13). This approach helps us keep a positive perspective when our homes start to look run down, we feel like we have nothing to wear, or our bank account is moving toward the red. When we focus on the unseen versus the seen (2 Corinthians 4:18), we discover enjoyment in nonmaterial pleasures like the smile on a friend's face, the hug of a loved one, or the satisfaction in a job well done.

The problem with getting our satisfaction from a purchase is the dopamine surge only lasts a moment. Our culture is built on the cycle of buying more to keep the dopamine flowing. As we grow older, we notice all the stuff we worked so hard to be able to buy is the same stuff we have to work to get rid of as we need to downsize. When we visit friends in assisted living or nursing homes, we see they live by a different set of values.

In John 10:10, Jesus said He came so we could live life to the full. True abundance is more than what we need. My father served as a missionary, and anytime I feel I lack something, I hear his words as he reflects on that experience. "The majority of Americans live like the kings and queens of the world." All it takes is a moment envisioning any child around the world living in poverty to remind ourselves we truly have an abundant life. We can place a photo of a child in poverty in our home to remind ourselves of our abundance. Our family has participated in the Compassion International Experience that allowed us to immerse ourselves in the world of child poverty.

When we notice a lack of something in our life, we can train our brain to rehearse three good things we have. I like to daily write down three unique things I'm grateful for that have occurred in the last 24 hours so I train my brain to be intentional and specific. What I notice is that this list rarely contains material items. I'm most grateful for the priceless things. I work with clients on the practice of being fully present in their day because this practice allows us to experience priceless moments easily missed. Training our brain to practice mindfulness by using all our senses will allow us to experience a deeper level of abundance. As we set our cell phones down more, inspect the faces of our loved ones, gaze into their eyes, listen for the sounds around us, hear our people laugh, and watch them move, these experiences bring overwhelming delight to our souls.

Asking "What can God do with ________?" reminds us He can do more than we can independently of Him. God can do more with $500 than I can. Asking this question when I look at my closet, inspires me to get creative. I keep an image of the bread loaves and fishes in my mind when I feel like there is no way I can stretch that far, give that much, or fulfill a certain calling. God taught me this when I got sick in the middle of a book launch one summer. God works while we rest. He is the door opener and doesn't need anything more than our obedience and availability.

Mindset Movement 1: *Choose a phase or Scripture that reminds you of the abundant life you've been given that you can say to yourself when you feel like you don't have enough. Look at your bank balance and say it. Then go to your closet and practice it there. Use your "abundance" verse when you are tempted to overspend or are feeling discontented about what we often call "first world problems." You may need to try a couple of phrases until you find the one that works for you.*

Mindset Movement 2: *The next time you are with people you treasure, practice mindfulness by activating all five of your senses—sight, sound, smell, touch, taste—so you are fully present.*

Chapter Eleven

The Victim Mindset—Battling Insecurity and Rejection

> "But you, God, see the trouble of the afflicted; you consider their grief and take it in hand. The victims commit themselves to you; you are the helper of the fatherless."
>
> —Psalm 10:14, NIV

"It's not my fault."

Ever said that? I have. And so have my kids, to infinity and beyond. Saying those words might grant a little relief in the moment as we try to escape culpability, shame, or rejection. But dodging blame will not rid us of a victim mindset. Shame can keep us bound in a victim mindset when we aren't willing to admit our need.

The psalmist knew all about victimhood. David was a victim many times over. But notice his path to victory started with a decision he made. He chose to surrender: "… The victims commit themselves to you …" (Psalm 10:14b, NIV). Surrender is the path to victory. Who knew? But David had to inform his belief system to be able to do so. By faith he knew God saw him and would help him.

The God Who Sees

David recognized God saw him. We can spiral into victimhood when we feel like no one sees or understands us. But the reality is God does see us; nothing is hidden from His sight. However, even though God sees us, this does not always mean we will get out of our situation. Regardless of our situation though, God will be with us.

Perhaps those words cause some of us to groan. We tend to think deliverance ought to mean a complete rescue. But what a witness it can be when we depend upon God for strength as we remain in the same circumstances yet walk in victory. In God's perfect timing and plan, if those circumstances should finally end, we discover we gained treasures even while we suffered. We are changed. Knowing the one true God is in control and sees us is a refuge when we are overwhelmed. The presence of God is our way out. Our path to victory is near. The reality that God sees us helps us view our circumstances and our victimhood through faith.

The God Who Considers

God considers us and the troubles we face. The word "consider" in Psalm 10:14 means to look intently at, to regard with favor, pleasure, or care, to have respect.[35] It means to see prophetically.[36] God looks at us with favor and care. He has a purpose for everything we go through. Nothing will be wasted. Do those words fly over your head or sink into your spirit?

The hurts of this life can wound our faith in God. When we struggle to believe God can help us, we need to remind ourselves with the truth of God's track record. He is incapable of failing. Our past, present, and future are all held in His capable hands. Sometimes we consider our trials to be burdens with no purpose. We just want deliverance. But God provides deliverance through the trials, not around them.

The God Who Helps

No circumstance we go through is beyond God's help. For the hopeless, He is our living Hope. For the helpless, He is our Helper through the Holy Spirit. And for the fatherless He is Abba Father.

I grew up with an ache for a father's love and for my daddy's attention and approval. I am not alone in this sadness. Sometimes we can intensify our own pain by our response. My dad and mom divorced when I was 12. Somehow, I knew they were going to drop the "D" word when they pulled my two brothers and me into the living room. I did not really understand what my parents getting divorced would mean for us, but I went numb. My grades tanked. I rarely saw my dad after that. My situation was hard. I moved eight times in the next nine years, attending various schools, one with gang fights on Fridays. But what was harder was staying stuck in victimhood because of it.

I did not know how to break free from my sorrow and the overwhelming pain that stemmed from the hardness of those years. I was extremely insecure and struggled greatly with rejection. But God. He saved me when I was 19 and in great need of His help. I wept for the better part of three years as God healed me and showed me He was the Dad that my dad couldn't be. My dad was not to blame; he did the best he could. His own battle with brokenness did not have to become mine. When I searched for the love of a father in the acceptance others, it only increased my pain resulting in rejection until I finally found the perfect Father. Forgiving our earthly fathers helps us to receive our Heavenly Father's love.

Victimhood Is a Prison

Victimhood keeps us bound in self and the fear of man, which causes insecurity and rejection. We dare not bust out of our prison for fear of what others might say or think. We adjust to the victim status and can wear our victimhood like an identity. Or maybe we are comfortable in our prison. We grow accustomed to being treated a certain way because of the scars we bear. In actuality, we might not even be aware we are acquiescing to victimhood. It might be all we know. But friends, the search for validation from man will never satisfy what the God of this universe has for us. Our identity is in Christ. He bore our victimhood on our behalf.

The Innocent Victim

Christ's sacrifice fulfilled what we could not. God came as the offering we could not afford to give. In the Book of Acts, Luke describes victims as the offerings for sins. In a history lesson to the religious leaders, courtesy of Stephen, Stephen tried to help them see their blindness and resistance to the Holy Spirit. He wanted them to recognize their need of God, to see what led to God's provision, and to understand what

Christ had accomplished on their behalf. Reciting from the book of Amos, Stephen showed how God's people had a divided heart. They thought they could worship both God and their little "gods," but the price for this sin was judgment from God. "But God turned away and gave them over to serve the heavenly lights; as it is written in the book of the prophets: 'You did not offer Me victims and sacrifices for forty years in the wilderness, did you, house of Israel?'" (Acts 7:42, NASB).

In love, God gave the Law to guide His people so they could know Him. The great chasm between God and man, between the Holy and the unholy, could be healed if man would just follow God's Law. But the Law revealed our great need and inability to uphold it. Man could not fulfill the demands of God's Law, so God provided again. He established a system whereby animals could be offered in man's place as required payment for sin. These offerings of animals in the old covenant are described as victims. Sin costs greatly. The wages of sin is death. All of us have to pay for our sins. But God decided to pay this debt for us. Christ became the victim on our behalf and bore our sins and victimhood. "For what the Law could not do, weak as it was through the flesh, God did: sending His own Son in the likeness of sinful flesh and as an offering for sin, He condemned sin in the flesh" (Romans 8:3, NASB).

We don't have to be a victim anymore. Christ bore our sins and sorrows. He has healed our waywardness, bore our pain, and lifted every burden we face. Will we let Him take our pain?

> "He was despised and abandoned by men, a man of great pain and familiar with sickness; and like one from whom people hide their faces, He was despised, and we had no regard for Him. How-

> ever, it was our sicknesses that He Himself bore, and our pains that He carried; yet we ourselves assumed that He had been afflicted, struck down by God, and humiliated. But He was pierced for our offenses, He was crushed for our wrongdoings; the punishment for our well-being was laid upon Him, and by His wounds we are healed" (Isaiah 53:3-5, NASB).

Christ understands what it is like to be mistreated, to be sick, to have pain. Like Jesus, our victimhood may be due to someone else's sin, and we are the ones who bear the consequences. It isn't fair. But then, what is fair is each of us paying for our own sins with our own lives. Somehow, we have to understand all of us will be victims at some point in this life at the hands of sinners exercising their free will, or just the result of living in a fallen world. Being a victim does not mean we have to remain one.

The key to getting out of the prison of victimhood is recognizing we don't have to be a victim anymore. We don't have to be defined by anything that happened to us as if it were an occupation or a family name. It's OK to let it go. We don't need that status anymore. We just need Jesus. And as we are healed, God can use us to help others who are bound in the prison of victimhood. Christ did not try to pay back those who insulted Him, beat Him, abused Him, and ultimately killed Him. He forgave them. This is the key to our freedom as well.

Operating from a Place of Wholeness

Those of us who have spent time in the victim mindset adopted some poor habits. We viewed others as enemies and centered everything around us and our pain. We don't have to do that anymore. God has our back. This will take time and some practice as we learn how to walk in the new freedom of not needing others to know we have experienced pain. In addition, we don't have to blame others for our pain anymore. We can choose to forgive the unforgiveable and walk in the grace that God has given.

Instead of assuming the motives of others from a position of brokenness, we can believe the best in people. And instead of thinking everyone does not like us, we can take the focus off our feelings of insecurity and rejection and place the focus on people who look like they need acceptance. When we walk in the Spirit instead of our victim flesh, we don't have the ball and chain of our hurts to drag alongside us. We are finally free to be who God made us to be as we let go of what enchained us.

A Note About Abuse Victims

For those of us who are victims of abuse, it is so hard to move past that kind of pain. Our very personhood was affected, and the anguish can last for years. I suffered abuse from a family member as a child. The nature of abuse silences victims, and I followed that abuse culture. I was told not to tell anyone, and I didn't. The silence kept the pain alive. For years I followed what I was told and did not tell a soul, and I got lost in that process. My soul was wounded and broken. Insecurity bred there as my worth, or lack of worth, was tied to what had happened to me. I felt dirty and unworthy. But then I met Jesus. I talked and prayed about the abuse as one who was pressing toward healing, not remaining in my hurt. And God healed me.

When we don't acknowledge the shame and hurt from the past, we cannot be healed. Hiding shame does not heal it. I made a vow that my children would not go through the same abuse I did and married a man who was a leader in the church. Later I discovered he wounded some of our children, too. In what became the biggest sorrow of my life and in the life of my children, healing has taken years and continues still. But rather than stay in unforgiveness, we are so grateful God graciously revealed the hidden sin and set us free.

Friends, broken people can abuse and harm people. The question burning in my soul was, "Can God heal this?" It felt too hard, too impossible. But God can heal, and He has. There are still moments where reminders cause pain or where another layer of healing happens. As my children and I recognize a behavior emanating from that abuse, we work through it. We can give ourselves space and grace as we process the awful stigmatizing pain from abuse. But we must tell ourselves the truth. What God says in His Word is true. And the lies that abuse casts on us don't have to stick anymore.

God does not want any of us to remain in an abusive situation. He can make a way out. God can change our story and bring us from glory to glory. "But we all, with unveiled faces, looking as in a mirror the glory of the Lord, are being transformed into the same image from glory to glory, just as from the Lord, the Spirit" (2 Corinthians 3:18, NASB). We can take hope from that word "all." None of us is defined by past abuse or failure. All who are in Christ are being restored and transformed. We can dare to believe God will do that. If He did it for me, He will do it for all. All of us are loved, and He made us all in His image. He swallows up all our grief and victim statuses and makes us new.

A Lesson from Paul: A Kingdom Mindset

If anyone knew what it was like to be a victim, it was Paul. He even boasted about his problems to illustrate the power of the grace of God for all who adopt the kingdom mindset, the mind of Christ.

> "Five times I received at the hands of the Jews the forty lashes less one. Three times I was beaten with rods. Once I was stoned. Three times I was shipwrecked; a night and a day I was adrift at sea; on frequent journeys, in danger from rivers, danger from robbers, danger from my own people, danger from Gentiles, danger in the city, danger in the wilderness, danger at sea, danger from false brothers; in toil and hardship, through many a sleepless night, in hunger and thirst, often without food, in cold and exposure. And, apart from other things, there is the daily pressure on me of my anxiety for all the churches. Who is weak, and I am not weak? Who is made to fall, and I am not indignant? If I must boast, I will boast of the things that show my weakness" (2 Corinthians 11:24-30, ESV).

I know we hate being told to compare ourselves to someone who has it worse than we do, but sometimes it brings perspective to our own suffering. Ultimately, comparing our suffering to others does not bring comfort. However, it wasn't comparing to others or avoiding hardships that gave Paul the victory. It was his mindset that was fixed on Christ and His purposes. A kingdom mentality made Paul think of his suffering in light of eternity rather than a temporary discomfort:

> "I want you to know, brothers, that what has happened to me has really served to advance the gospel, so that it has become known throughout the whole imperial guard and to all the rest that my imprisonment is for Christ. And most of the brothers, having become confident in the Lord by my imprisonment, are much more bold to speak the word without fear" (Philippians 1:12-13, ESV).

What's Paul saying? Good can come from his victimhood? Yes. This is what happens in God's economy. When we don't respond as victims but as victors because of God's grace, people see God at work in us. We don't need their pity. When we keep a proper perspective amid our suffering—a perspective focused on spiritual reality, not physical—we overcome, just like Paul did and like so many of God's other servants in Scripture.

We overcome just like Christ did, too. This is the heritage of those of us who are in Christ. We can see beyond our circumstances and live for Christ even in the worst of times. Truly, especially during suffering, we are a witness to others. Like Paul, we are more than conquerors. In our weakness we are strong. We are empowered from on high and no longer victims.

One Mind

Sometimes there is a victim mentality in group settings. There can be as many ways to be offended as there are people, it seems. We can be so easily divided. Offenses can impact churches, families, and workplaces with all the different political views and related hurt feelings. It's a wonder anything can be accomplished with all the drama from given mindsets in group settings. But Paul invited us to embrace one mindset, the same mind, the mind of Christ: "Only let your manner of life be worthy of the gospel of Christ, so that whether I come and see you or am absent, I may hear of you that you are standing firm in one spirit, with one mind striving side by side for the faith of the gospel" (Philippians 1:27, ESV).

The enemy of our souls uses our mindsets against us. If he can get us to stall out and be stuck in any of the mindsets, it destroys unity in the Church, unity at home, and unity in our relationships. Mindsets are strongholds fueled by lies. We must pray to recognize them and not give in to them. When we all have the mind of Christ, we stand in agreement and avoid a lot of drama.

Trigger 1: It's All About Me

Pity parties are birthed when the focus is on us. Certainly, we can have compassion for our suffering. However, if we keep in mind that when we don't avoid problems but persevere through them, we can use the experience to gain character.

When people tell us to "Suck it up, buttercup," that charges the victim mentality even more, right? That's not a very compassionate way to encourage someone who is suffering. However, sometimes we might need a reminder to take the focus off self. James has some advice for fellow sufferers: "Consider it pure joy, my brothers and sisters, whenever you face trials of many kinds, because you know that the testing of your faith produces perseverance" (James 1:2-3, NIV). This is not an uncompassionate verse; it is a heads-up that we will all suffer, and it's an encouragement that none of our suffering will be wasted.

Complaining about our suffering will not heal us. Focusing on our pain will overwhelm us. But dealing with our suffering, whether it is physical or mental, by processing our struggles with Scripture, helps us to overcome. For each struggle we can find and embrace an accompanying verse. God will amaze us when we rely on Him and His precious Word.

Trigger 2: "It's Not Fair!"

The temptation to give in to the victim mindset is sometimes relentless. We can feel our burden is unfair. But comparing our suffering to others' suffering just incites a victim response. Besides, how do we measure fairness and suffering? Our definition of fairness is skewed toward self. God makes a way out when we are tempted to stay stuck in victimhood. "The temptations in your life are no different from what others experience. And God is faithful. He will not allow the temptation to be more than you can stand. When you are tempted, he will show you a way out so that you can endure" (1 Corinthians 10:13, NLT). The faithfulness of God is our hope, not the absence of pain.

Trigger 3: Stop Fighting

Sometimes we sink into the victim mindset because we don't see a way out of it. We fight the cause of our victimhood, but we don't fight the victim mentality. Then we just get more entrenched in that pit. Maybe when there seems to be no hope and everything feels against us, we should stop fighting. That's right. We should stop being resentful about the suffering and start fighting the spiritual battle instead. Why? When the God of this universe is for us, who can be against us (Romans 8:31)? Friends, God fights our battles for us. "For the LORD your God is the one who goes with you to fight for you against your enemies to give you victory" (Deuteronomy 20:4, NIV). Will we be patient enough to wait on God for His deliverance? Will we trust Him and have faith in His ability to rescue us?

Trigger 4: Take Responsibility

Situations do not become easier by avoiding responsibility. When we are accountable for our part in our pain, we learn from it. Holding on to every injustice or hurt just ends up hurting us all over again. Instead of trying to make someone else responsible for our victim status, we can forgive and recognize people often operate in brokenness. These actions set us free from remaining stuck as a victim.

We may never hear offenders say they are truly sorry for the pain they caused. They may never accept their responsibility even though it is theirs to bear before Almighty God. But we can let God deal with them and move on with our life. They took enough of our life and energy. We don't have to let them take anymore.

Trigger 5: Rejection

One of the most painful things in my life has been rejection. The human soul wants to be known—and accepted. When others victimize us by rejecting us, our insecurities can feed into our victim status. Jesus has an interesting solution to those hateful toward us. Love them anyway. This feels impossible in our flesh, but with the mind of Christ, which we have, we can go against our flesh and walk in the Spirit. "But I say to you who hear, love your enemies, do good to those who hate you, bless those who curse you, pray for those who are abusive to you" (Luke 6:27-28, NASB).

A Victor in Christ

Being a victim is easy. Many people will help us do that. But it is also incredibly hard to be a victim and do anything else that's positive. We become a prisoner to our status in our own minds. The victory is already ours through Christ. However, we need to reach for it and let go of the victim status we let define us. We don't need the sympathy of others. We are blessed with every spiritual blessing in Christ. We are a victor in Christ.

Tip 1: Perspective

Noticing someone else's suffering has a way of putting ours into perspective. Many times people have told me they gained perspective on their problems when they became aware of mine. But true perspective is not gained from comparison. It is gained from looking through the eyes of Jesus and seeing our lives in the scope of eternity. We gain perspective in our suffering by recognizing what we really deserve and didn't get. We gain godly perspective when we remember Jesus chose the suffering we seek to avoid. We don't have to stay in our suffering anymore.

I know this can be so hard to grasp because sometimes we are physically still experiencing horrors on this earth. But there is a place in our mind where we can go to find refuge: the mind of Christ. Having His perspective on our suffering helps us to no longer see things dimly. When we see what Christ did on our behalf, we can only be grateful. Perhaps we can even recognize there is purpose in our suffering. Even the most awful suffering we encounter can be repurposed by our awesome God.

Our view of suffering is quite different from ages gone by. God flat out told Paul he would suffer. "And I will show him how much he must suffer for my name's sake" (Acts 9:16, NLT). I am pretty sure none of us wants to read that in our job description. But Christ showed us how to suffer. He knew what His suffering was achieving. "For Christ also suffered once for sins, the righteous for the unrighteous, to bring you to God. He was put to death in the body but made alive in the Spirit" (1 Peter 3:18, NIV). Our suffering does not take Christ by surprise. He is enough for every sorrow we encounter.

Tip 2: Expectations

Failed expectations can leave us disillusioned. Most of us don't start out on a path expecting trouble, but perhaps the troubles we seek to avoid can work toward our deliverance. David was a witness to this truth: "Though you have made me see troubles, many and bitter, you will restore my life again; from the depths of the earth you will again bring me up" (Psalm 71:20, NIV).

The God who allowed the psalmist to see troubles, to experience harsh suffering, was the same God the psalmist looked to for restoration. David knew he was not blameless, and neither did he blame God. We often do that today, don't we? We revel in our victim status sometimes to get attention. We blame others for our suffering due to their broken promises or harsh treatment. But in reality, we don't have to play or stay the victim. One expectation will never fail us: We can look to God for restoration. We don't need to look to ourselves or others to remove our pain.

Tip 3: Stay on Mission

I learned a beautiful lesson about how mindsets can be transformed as I lay down my victimhood and picked up my identity in Christ. As I lay in the hospital bed, hooked up to oxygen, a heart monitor, and two IVs—because the phlebotomist was new—victimhood was rising within my soul. My body temperature had plummeted with the onset of possible sepsis, and different infections spawned from my multisystem inflammatory syndrome. I could not see my husband or anyone else due to the crackdown against COVID. My husband drove around the hospital parking lot, hoping he could find my hospital room and catch a glimpse of me. He could not bring me an anniversary card or smuggle in a Bible because of the fear of germs.

But my husband could text me a picture of his precious card and have me translate his French, which I know he wrote using Google Translate, just sayin'. Even though asthma and COVID made it hard for me to talk, we could still read the card and cry together between my asthmatic gasps for air. *But* my husband could also read through several Scriptures over the phone with me, and we agreed together.

During that time my husband's mom was in the final season of her life on this earth. COVID prevented him from seeing her or me. *But* we were able to call her on the phone. I had the chance to weep with my husband's parents and thank them for accepting me into their family. Hours would go by before I saw a soul because entering my room required so much preparation due to my COVID diagnosis. So I wept, and I prayed. I felt so unseen and uncared for. *But* God.

Did you catch all of those "buts"? Victimhood was trying to win, but I made a choice to let go of victimhood and asked God to help me see His goodness through it all. By the grace of God, I had a mindset overhaul as God reminded me that I had much to be grateful for and I was on mission. Instead of being upset with the health-care workers, I asked God to help me think about them and how hard it must be to deal with COVID. Instead of lamenting over my suffering, I asked God to show me His purposes for me in that suffering.

Friends, our pain points are a mission, should we choose to accept it. Rather than being a victim, we can look around and ask God whom we are supposed to reach. As I started to care for the health-care workers, they began to share their burdens with me. Then I shared Jesus with them, too. Having compassion on them helped me to let go of the victim status and become a victor in that place.

Yes, it was super hard. I had to wash my hair in a sink (probably wasn't supposed to do that) and walk around my room to make my heart rate go up to get some assistance (probably wasn't supposed to do that either). But when hard times come, we see what we are made of: flesh or the Spirit—

and lots of grit. Victory is chosen, friends, right in the middle of the hard. Having compassion on others gives us patience and understanding in our struggles.

Tip 4: Be Strong

If we tell people to be strong in their own strength when they are knee-deep in victimhood, it just makes them more of a victim. The strength we need to get out of our victimhood is available to us, but we must know how to access it. Paul reminds us where this strength lies. "Finally, be strong in the Lord and in his mighty power" (Ephesians 6:10, NIV).

We don't have to be strong in our own strength. We just need to be strong in our faith, trusting in Jesus' mind and power, not our own. We access this strength by admitting our weaknesses and crying out to God. Then we demonstrate it by believing God is able, and He keeps His promises. "For everyone born of God overcomes the world. This is the victory that has overcome the world, even our faith" (1 John 5:4, NIV). And when our faith is as small as a mustard seed, God supplies our need then, too.

Tip 5: Others-Focused

Our deepest pains can produce the deepest compassion within us. Comforting others with the comfort we have received takes the focus off ourselves and uses our suffering for good purposes. Rather than focusing on our problems, our personal insecurities, or our rejection, we can go to God about them. God is not against comfort. He wants to be our comfort. But amazingly, our own hurts seem to diminish as we care about what others are going through instead of our own burdens.

Getting to the Root

We weren't made to be victims. Sin did that. But Christ came to bear all our shame and pain to restore our identity in Him. We don't have to identify with our victimhood any longer. We don't have to let rejection or insecurities keep us from the abundant life the mind of Christ offers. We are accepted, friends. We will never be more accepted because of our works. Nor will we be rejected by our Savior when we bring all our hurts and sorrows to Him. We can cast our burdens on Him. He cares for us.

Mindset of Christ

Christ chose to be a victim on our behalf, but He did not choose victimhood. We don't have to live in a victim mentality. Christ showed us how to counter rejection, abuse, and insults. "When they hurled their insults at him, he did not retaliate; when he suffered, he made no threats. Instead, he entrusted himself to him who judges justly" (1 Peter 2:23, NIV). Christ countered victimhood with surrender. He trusted the Father and His will.

Mind Renewal: Keys to Unlock Our Mind

Key Thought:

When our mind is set on God's will, we are no longer a victim but a servant of the most high God.

Key Verse: Truth from God's Word

"But thanks be to God, who gives us the victory through our Lord Jesus Christ" (1 Corinthians 15:57, ESV).

Key Change: Application—Releasing Our Victim Status and Choosing Victory

It is hard to face our pain and walk through it; however, that's the only path to healing. Take some time to pray and think about moments in your life when you were a victim. Search for Scriptures specific to your situation. Speak that truth over your life and ask God to help you recognize lies in the victim status. Write down what the Holy Spirit reveals to you and how you can think about things differently.

Counselor's Corner

Most good stories have the following characters: a hero, a villain, and a victim. When we watch a movie or read a book, we enjoy following this "drama triangle"; it's entertaining. For counselors treating people who have been abused, a major goal is to get them out of the victim, rescuer, perpetrator triangle. I see it all the time in families. A child with a bad temper hurts a brother or sister. The parent comes to the rescue of the wounded child but then loses it with the original perpetrator, making that child a victim of the parent.

How do we help families get out of these never-ending triangles? First, we put safety plans in place that usually involve separation and supervision. Next, we work at reducing the intensity of all the emotions in the family. Finally, we help people discover new roles. Parents who are used to playing the hero become the coach. Children who would lash out physically begin to use their words and ask for time-outs. People who have been hurt choose not to take revenge but rather ask themselves questions like:

"What can God teach me from this experience?"

"How do I see God using this for good in my life?"

"What could I do differently to avoid this type of situation in the future?"

Leaving the victim mindset behind involves focusing on what we can change—ourselves—and letting go of what we can't change—other people. This approach gets us out of the blame game and creates powerful energy for change. Family counselors bear witness that it only takes one person to change her role to impact relationship dynamics. The system will fight to remain the same, but when we refuse to be who we've always been, we cause positive change. The help of a trained outsider can also be useful. Family counselors work hard to stay outside the triangle so they can help everyone find a way out.

Mindset Movement 1: *Identify which roles in the drama triangle you tend to take on.*

Mindset Movement 2: *The next time you feel like a victim, ask yourself, "What can I learn from this experience?" Changing from victim to learner breaks you out of the drama triangle.*

Chapter Twelve

The Mind of Christ

"For, 'Who has known the mind of the Lord so as to instruct him?' But we have the mind of Christ."
—1 Corinthians 2:16, NIV

When he was a kid, my oldest son used to think he might have superpowers. He could scale a wall and had reflexes like I had never seen. And his mind, one of his choir directors used to say, was like a raccoon's, razor sharp. At a young age my son recognized there was potential beyond what he was experiencing. Some people are deep, critical thinkers like that. He wondered what would happen if people could use all their brain, since purportedly humans use only 10 percent of their brain capacity. (Dale Carnegie's 1936 book, *How to Win Friends and Influence People,* referenced the 10 percent figure, but this has widely been viewed as a myth.) Then one day my son discovered he did not truly have "superpowers" but "supernatural" ones. He could understand spiritual things, and he could have the mind of Christ. We all can, friends. But not all of us choose to.

The Power of Repentance

For the created to have the mind of the Creator is a miracle indeed. God's thoughts are not our thoughts, yet we can have the mind of Christ. How? Simply put, we can have Christ's mind if we repent and believe. In the Gospel of Mark, Jesus' first recorded spoken words involved changing our mindset. "The time is fulfilled, and the kingdom of God is at hand; repent and believe in the gospel" (Mark 1:15, NASB). Repentance is first, then believing.

Satan's chief tactic is to deceive us, to distract us so we will not repent. For believers, Satan wants to keep us in turmoil, so we are ineffective. This is one reason why our belief system is under so much attack. If we can be distracted by various negative mindsets, we'll be trapped, then it feels impossible to overcome them. But God.

For those of us who are in Christ and still struggling with negative mindsets, these words "repent" and "believe" are still the key for us, as well. Repentance is not a one-time act. The words "repent"[37] and "repentance"[38] occur approximately 130 times in Scripture. This indicates we need to hear about and actually repent more than once. As we become aware of our sinful negative mindsets, we need to repent and ask Christ to change us. Repent in the Greek is *metanoéō*. It means to change one's mind, to amend with abhorrence of one's past sins.[39] This conveys an about-face; we spin 180 degrees and go the opposite direction. Repentance does not coexist with lukewarm faith. It leads to radical transformation.

The word "believe" is the Greek word *pisteúō*. It means to have saving faith, to think to be true, to be persuaded of, to commit or put trust in. This word is "used in the NT of the conviction and trust to which a man is impelled by a certain inner and higher prerogative and law of soul."[40] In a few cases in Scripture we see the Greek word for mindset combined with the verb *epistrepsas*, meaning to turn around. "This refers to the bringing back of the erring member by the Christian brother.[41]

Friends, we never arrive down here. We will need to battle mindsets the rest of our days. But when we are equipped to counter them and be aware of their presence, we can walk in freedom. The threefold process is easy to remember. They all start with the letter "R"—typically expressed as R^3 or R-cubed.

- Recognize the mindset.
- Repent of the sin involved in the mindset.
- Return to the mind of Christ.

We can't put confidence in our own mindset. We must lay it down. We cannot hold on to our perspective and expect to have Christ's. We are never above the need to repent. Mindsets are sinful strongholds, and they need to be put in their place.

When I accepted Christ back in 1988, everything changed. I read the Bible straight through in the first three years after my salvation and many years afterward. I changed the music I listened to. I stopped dating. These radical changes came about because my heart compelled me to repent and follow Jesus, not to live in my former ways anymore. Over 30 years later I still have my "come to Jesus" moments when I realize I have drifted some in my thinking. Staying in God's Word helps me to see this. The Holy Spirit illumines my need. We just have to ask God to help our stubborn, hard hearts turn back to Him. We should never believe the lie that we can't change. We can overcome the negative mindsets of this world, and it begins with repentance and placing our faith in Jesus.

As we look over the landscape of the body of Christ today, the question remains: If we have the mind of Christ, why are many not walking in it? The influences of the kingdom of the air are strong. Our mindsets can be turned in a moment. The fruit of negative mindsets is readily seen in the backbiting and gossiping and other carnal behaviors that are all too rampant in churches (1 Corinthians 3:3). Worldliness elbows out godliness. But accessing the mind of Christ is not something we can do; it is something Christ has already done. Hollow worldly thoughts can easily take us captive and distract us from what is already ours. Putting off and putting on Christ's thoughts is a daily battle, but we can cultivate the mind of Christ and let go of the carnal mentality.

The Mind or Heart?

There are additional words that the Bible uses to describe our mindset. The alternation of *dianoia,* or mind, and *kardia,* heart, shows that both are synonymously related to the center of man's inner life.[42] These concepts illustrate how important our heart and mind are in the way we live. What begins in our thoughts translates into actions. "But what comes out of the mouth proceeds from the heart (*kardia*), and this defiles a person" (Matthew 15:18, ESV). We must get things right in our heart from the start. Our mindset is the determining factor. Our mindset is how we decide to process our thoughts. We are likely unaware of this choice because most of our thought life has become so automated.

This Is a "Put-On"

This world has so many faulty solutions. We just want peace, but we try to find it in places that cannot deliver. There are so many "put-ons" in this world that leave us feeling jaded and weary. But in the end, we are called to put on the mind of Christ. As we read the words below from Paul, we can understand what we need to do.

> "Now this I say and testify in the Lord, that you must no longer walk as the Gentiles do, in the futility of their minds. They are darkened in their understanding, alienated from the life of God because of the ignorance that is in them, due to their hardness of heart. They have become callous and have given themselves up to sensuality, greedy to practice every kind of impurity. But that is not the way you learned Christ!—assuming that you have heard about him and were taught in him, as the truth is in Jesus, to put off your old self, which belongs to your former manner of life and is corrupt through deceitful desires, and to be renewed in the spirit of your minds, and to put on the new self, created after the likeness of God in true righteousness and holiness" (Ephesians 4:17-24, ESV).

We cannot put on if we have not first put off. And we do not know what we need to put off without having a plumb line. We need to continually renew our mind with God's perspective (the mind of Christ) to be able to let go of the world's perspective. There is a battle of mindsets all around us. Not recognizing these battles will only serve to take us captive. But we need to know how to fight. Paul recognized the need to fight with the right weapons: "We use God's mighty weapons, not worldly weapons, to knock down the strongholds of human reasoning and to destroy false arguments" (2 Corinthians 10:4, NLT). Human reasoning and mindsets are a stronghold. They are a trap that keeps us from living in the mind of Christ and living the abundant life Christ promises.

We can't underestimate someone's mindset. Mindsets can lead people to do things they would not normally do. The battle is spiritual, not in the flesh. We need to fight it spiritually. And the Bible is our plumb line, not more human reasoning. "We destroy arguments and every lofty opinion raised against the knowledge of God, and take every thought captive to obey Christ" (2 Corinthians 10:5, ESV). When we consider our fleshly mindsets are against the knowledge of God, we realize the importance of being set free from the world's mentality. Man's opinions are counter to God's mind and His knowledge. We can sometimes stay stuck in mindset wars because we want to be proved right. That is a fleshly perspective. Caring more about God's glory and His perspective is what we need to be set free.

Mindset Matters

When our mind is controlled, it then affects our actions. As we are diligent to put on the mind of Christ, the application of that mindset reflects in how we think and act. It's a battle with our flesh. That is the expectation. But we dare not rest from the pursuit of holiness. There is no neutral, friends. We are either moving forward or backward. The good news is we have the

Helper, the precious Holy Spirit, who enables us to have the mind of Christ and to walk in it.

> "Those who live according to the flesh have their minds set on what the flesh desires; but those who live in accordance with the Spirit have their minds set on what the Spirit desires. The mind governed by the flesh is death, but the mind governed by the Spirit is life and peace. The mind governed by the flesh is hostile to God; it does not submit to God's law, nor can it do so. Those who are in the realm of the flesh cannot please God" (Romans 8:5-8, NIV).

Noted theologian Douglas Moo wrote the following about these verses: "The word for mindset is found in the Greek word *phronema* that Paul uses in verse 5. It might best be rendered as 'mindset.' … These words include intellectual activity ('thinking' in the narrow sense) but go beyond it to involve the will also. The *phronema* is our fundamental orientation, the convictions and heart attitude that steers the course of our life."[43] As it says in Proverbs 4:23, "Guard your heart above all else, for it determines the course of your life" (NLT).

It is the Holy Spirit's job to develop the mindset of Christ within us, but we cooperate as we saturate our mind in His Word and ask for Him to give us understanding. We can't just let ourselves remain stuck in negative mindsets. We don't have to anymore. How we think matters and affects our whole life, as well as the lives of others. More than that, when we give ourselves over to negative mindsets, Paul says we are hostile toward God, the One who made us, loves us, and gave

His life for us. Friends, hostility is hatred. The enemy of our souls wants to get our minds opposed to God. That is what negative mindsets do. Mere positivity or trying in our own strength will not change our mind. Only the mind of Christ will. When Peter tried to rebuke Jesus by placing his thoughts above God's, Jesus put Peter in his place (Matthew 16:23). We must have the things of God and His thoughts above our own.

What is the Mind of Christ?

The mind of Christ is God's thoughts born out in our lives by the power of the Holy Spirit. This happens as we renew our mind with God's Word and examine our thoughts to line up with His. We have been indoctrinated by the world's system all our days. It will take time to learn a mindset reset and adopt the mind of Christ. Christ set the example of what it looks like to live into God's thoughts instead of man's. We have seen how Christ responded when faced with the same negative mindsets we experience. Long before Jesus lived among us, He was. He has always been. The Old Testament tells of His coming, and the New Testament tells of His coming again. All of Scripture says look to the Son.

We have seen the mind of Christ "fleshed out" for us to understand how to counter negative mindsets. We understand from Scripture that we have this mind within us. We don't have to think in the flesh anymore by giving in to negative mindsets. The Mind of Christ is the goal but not the means. The Holy Spirit helps us in this transformation. But sometimes we struggle to access what we already have. We must make up our mind to think like Christ. It will take some time to form new habits, especially with the negative mindsets we struggle with the most. But the mind of Christ is more than a habit. It is walking in the Spirit and resisting the flesh. It is asking God for wisdom and discernment, casting aside the old and putting on the new. The Holy Spirit gives us the mind of Christ.

> "These are the things God has revealed to us by his Spirit. The Spirit searches all things, even the deep things of God. ... The person with the Spirit makes judgments about all things, but such a person is not subject to merely human judgments, for, 'Who has known the mind of the Lord so as to instruct him?' But we have the mind of Christ" (1 Corinthians 2:10-16, NIV).

The Holy Spirit is often neglected as we walk out our faith, but it is the Holy Spirit who works within us to give us understanding and to help us to think like Christ. Long before Jesus came in the likeness of our flesh, Isaiah wrote about the sevenfold aspects of the Holy Spirit that would be upon the promised Messiah. It is the same Holy Spirit who was with Christ who is also with us today. Conceived of the Spirit (Luke 1:35), Jesus also had the Spirit descend upon Him (Luke 3:22). The Holy Spirit, the third person of the Trinity, descended upon Jesus in the fullness of His influences, and produced in Christ the beautiful character we see in Him, the mind of Christ. Christ walked among us, fully God and fully man, indwelt by the Holy Spirit, which operated in the mind of Christ and can operate in our minds, too.

A Lesson from the Holy Spirit: The Sevenfold Spirit of God

When I was a kid, I liked to watch shows where the character had some secret power. Most of us would like to possess a feeling of might that enables us to overcome. Yet sometimes we do not let the Holy Spirit exercise power in our life. We quench the Spirit and follow the flesh instead. The Holy Spirit is God. God is triune. While this blows our minds, Scripture gives us insight into this mysterious sevenfold mind of the Spirit, as shown below:

> "There shall come forth a Rod from the stem of Jesse, And a Branch shall grow out of his roots. The Spirit of the LORD shall rest upon Him, The Spirit of wisdom and understanding, The Spirit of counsel and might, The Spirit of knowledge and of the fear of the LORD. His delight is in the fear of the LORD, And He shall not judge by the sight of His eyes, Nor decide by the hearing of His ears; But with righteousness He shall judge the poor, And decide with equity for the meek of the earth;" (Isaiah 11:1-4a, NKJV).

Spirit of the Lord

The Holy Spirit rested on Jesus and dwells within us. He enables us to have the mind of Christ. The Hebrew word for Spirit is *rûwach,* which means Spirit of God, the third person of the triune God, mind, disposition of mind or attitude, seat of emotion.[44] Before we know God, the Holy Spirit reveals the things of God and convicts us of wrong thinking. "When he comes, he will prove the world to be in the wrong about sin and righteousness and judgment" (John 16:8, NIV). The Holy Spirit guides us to think like Christ.

Spirit of Wisdom

The Spirit of wisdom is God's perfect thoughts. The Holy Spirit gives us His wisdom and insight. God promises to give wisdom to everyone, but we need to ask. "If any of you lacks wisdom, you should ask God, who gives generously to all without finding fault, and it will be given to you" (James 1:5, NIV).

Spirit of Understanding

The Holy Spirit illumines our minds to help us understand the things of God. Encased in flesh, we struggle to understand God's ways. But with God all things are possible. "But it was to us that God revealed these things by His Spirit. For his Spirit searches out everything and shows us God's deep secrets" (1 Corinthians 2:10, NLT). But God wants more than just a mere academic understanding or knowing about God. He invites the unholy to become holy and to understand His ways, too.

Spirit of Counsel

God guides us and instructs us how to think rightly. "But the Advocate, the Holy Spirit, whom the Father will send in my name, will teach you all things and will remind you of everything I have said to you" (John 14:26, NIV). The Holy Spirit is our Counselor.

Spirit of Might

Living out the mind of Christ is done by the strength of God. What a display of God's greatness to see people walking in the Spirit of God rather than the flesh. When we consider our weakness, it is a miracle indeed. "I can do all things through Him who strengthens me" (Philippians 4:13, NASB).

Spirit of Knowledge

Wisdom is knowledge applied. Evidence of the mindset of Christ in our life is bearing out that knowledge. God's thoughts are not our thoughts. His ways are not our ways, but the Holy Spirit opens our eyes to understand. "That the God of our Lord Jesus Christ, the Father of glory, may give you the Spirit of wisdom and of revelation in the knowledge of him, having the eyes of your hearts enlightened, that you may know what is the hope to which he has called you, what are the riches of his glorious inheritance in the saints" (Ephesians 1:17-18, ESV).

Fear of the Lord

We demonstrate what we say we believe. The mind of Christ impacts our obedience to God. Fearing God might sound like a strange concept. We don't think of fearing someone we love. But knowledge of God includes the understanding that He is holy. When we stand in reverence and awe of God, we are more apt to walk in the Spirit rather than the flesh. Scripture tells us that fearing God is where true knowledge begins. "The fear of the Lord is the beginning of knowledge;

fools despise wisdom and instruction" (Proverbs 1:7, ESV). I made this verse reference part of my personal email address. I want to be reminded of it every day.

Many years ago, a friend asked me to write her daughter a letter describing the most important thing in my walk with God. After praying about it, I wrote that the fear of the Lord has been the biggest blessing of my life. The fear of God helps us to resist sin, and it reminds us of how awesome our God is.

Why We Need to Think Like Jesus

When we are beset with negative mindsets, we need to remember how Jesus countered them. Christ exemplified what it means to walk in the Spirit even though He was in the flesh. He had the mind of the Spirit and demonstrated it with perfect humility, holiness, wisdom, and selflessness. Through torture, temptation, abuse, persecution, gossip, and shame, Jesus walked blamelessly. He blazed the trail before us and showed us how to rise above the carnal mindsets that are so prevalent.

We need to think like Jesus so negative mindsets will not affect our walk with God. Negative mindsets are a spiritual stronghold that prevent us from living the victorious life Christ accomplished on the cross and through His resurrection power. We don't have to live just for this world. It will leave us empty.

We need to think like Jesus because we are His witnesses and testimonies of what God can do with our brokenness. Walking in the flesh is a poor witness that does not represent Christ well. It is a stumbling block for others seeking the grace we found.

We need to think like Jesus to please God. How can the unrighteous please a righteous God? The amazing thing about the mind of Christ is it's for anyone. It's not only for smart people or for the high and lofty. It is for the beggar in the street, the housewife, the child. It is for everyone who believes. But the mind of the flesh cannot know the thoughts of God.

We need to think like Jesus so we can obey God. The greatest commandment is not optional, yet even this we cannot do without God's help. "And you shall love the Lord your God with all your heart and with all your soul and with all your mind and with all your strength" (Mark 12:30, ESV). That word "all" is intimidating. Our thoughts can be so scattered that the thought of using all our mind to love God seems impossible. But the more we fill our mind with the things of God, the more we can love God.

Friends, if we don't have the mind of Christ, our mind can become a playhouse for the devil. Entertaining the different mindsets is torture and impacts our belief system. We will not stay on the mission God has for us if we are not vigilant with the thoughts in our mind. We must continually choose the mind of Christ instead of our own.

Steps to Thinking Like Jesus

We have seen what the mind of Christ is, how it operates, and our need of it. But still, we might struggle to access the mind of Christ. Even though there may not be a formal procedure or a quick good work we can do to connect with Christ's mind easy-peasy, there are principles to guide us and steps we can take. Peter and Paul emphasized the condition of our mindset on several occasions. Peter even said it was the very purpose for writing both of his letters. "I have written both of them as reminders to stimulate you to wholesome thinking" (2 Peter 3:1b, NIV). Walking in Jesus' footsteps and mindset will mean studying to know His heart and thoughts. Peter gave us a few pointers in this regard in his first letter:

> "Therefore, prepare your minds for action, keep sober in spirit, set your hope completely on the grace to be brought to you at the revelation of Jesus Christ. As obedient children, do not be conformed to the former lusts which were yours in your ignorance, but like the Holy One who called you, be holy yourselves also in all your behavior" (1 Peter 1:13-15, NASB).

Step 1: Prepare Our Minds for Action

We must realize that reigning in our thoughts is a battle and prepare our minds for this truth. Just because we are not aware of a battle does not mean it is not being waged against us. It will take practice to learn how to adjust our mindset from the world's to that of Christ's.

Step 2: Keep Sober in Spirit

A sober spirit does not mean walking in the Spirit is not fun. However, if we are not careful, we can be lulled into frivolity and a lack of self-control. Our flesh does not like living a disciplined life. The spiritual disciplines help keep us focused so we do not give in to the negative mindsets that can cause us to live an ungodly life. When we are self-aware, we can resist the negative mindsets.

Step 3: Reset Our Hope

Our hopes can lead us astray. When we hope in this world, we will be let down. That's a sure bet. The human condition is the impetus for hope. There has got to be something better, right? This is not Heaven down here, and we will need to surrender our own hopes to find real, lasting hope. If this feels like a kind of death, it is. But in Christ, we no longer live, but Christ lives in us. That means we must lay down our agendas. If we could understand the hope that God has for us, we would not hold on to our hope for one second longer. We can trust God. He is our living hope.

Step 4: Be Obedient

We cannot blame personalities or circumstances or other people for our struggle with various negative mindsets. Well, we can, but it won't help us overcome them. We have a choice. It will be a struggle, but we must tell ourselves the truth and ignore the lies of the enemy. We can choose to obey God and to adopt a new mindset rather than the tired, fleshly mindsets of the world.

Step 5: Be Holy

Adapting to the new creation we are in Christ will take some convincing of our mindset, which is naturally bent on the flesh, not the Spirit. As we go through the sanctification process, we can know that the One who called us is holy, and He will complete the work He began in us (Philippians 1:6). But He would not tell us to be holy if we did not have a part in living that out. As we abide in the Spirit, we will have to say no to negative mindsets from walking in the flesh. "Since we live by the Spirit, let us keep in step with the Spirit" (Galatians 5:25, NIV).

A Stolen Identity

Having the mind of Christ is hard to do when we seek to find our identity in other things, positions, relationships, achievements, or anything other than who we are in relationship with God. When we let negative mindsets hijack us, we are giving into an identity. For instance, when someone labels us, boastful pride may rise up to defend ourselves or we acquiesce to that label. But the mind of Christ responds differently.

When we know who we are in Christ, we don't need to wrestle with the philosophies of this world. We don't have to try to prove or defend ourselves anymore. God has our back. When our identity is firmly in Christ, the negative mindsets don't govern us as much anymore. We belong. We don't have to be angry or depressed when things don't go a certain way because we know God's purposes for us are good.

Having One Mind

The Apostle Paul pleaded with the people of God to adopt the same mindset—the mind of Christ—in order to have unity in the Church. "Complete my joy by being of the same mind, having the same love, being in full accord and of one mind" (Philippians 2:2, ESV). Negative mindsets create disunity. The only path to unity is for all believers to lay down, or crucify, the flesh, its desires, and mentalities and to adopt the mind of Christ. This is what creates unity in the body of Christ: one Lord and one mind focused on God's glory, not ours. As we each seek to live in the mind of Christ and not give in to the negative mindsets, we can help change the culture around us. All things are possible through Christ.

Living Out the Mind of Christ

The Apostle John shared a sweet promise about obtaining a mind like Christ's: "And we know that the Son of God has come and has given us understanding, so that we may know him who is true; and we are in him who is true, in his Son Jesus Christ. He is the true God and eternal life" (1 John 5:20, ESV). John's emphasis on Jesus being true is significant. The negative mindsets scream lies to us, and we have heard them so long we do not question them. Jesus has given understanding. The work is finished. We have been redeemed and given the mind of Christ. We just have to learn to live into it.

This word "understanding" is not based on our ability to understand, but on Christ's ability to help us see things through His pure, eternal mindset. Noted theologians Behm and Würthwein said the use of the word understanding here is an orientation of our mind that Christ does. "The Son of God has awakened in us the mind and given our thinking the orientation to know God, to receive His revelation, to share fellowship with Him.[45] Why do so many of us not have this understanding? Various triggers stand in the way of us accessing the mind of Christ.

Trigger 1: Aligning Our Thoughts

We are used to listening to ourselves and don't question the legitimacy of our thoughts because they are our own. But believing in ourselves is a mistake. We need to adjust our minds to God's Word and align our thoughts—which require a constant calibration—to God's thoughts. Now if this sounds like work, it is. But like anything, the more we do it, the more natural it becomes. We are not stuck in a mindset just because "that is the way we have always been" or because it's a part of our culture. Jesus can help us understand. "Then He opened their minds to understand the Scriptures" (Luke 24:45, NASB). We must press in, friends, to know God and to understand His Word. God's Word is living and faithful. "Whoever trusts in his own mind is a fool, but he who walks in wisdom will be delivered" (Proverbs 28:26, ESV).

Trigger 2: Habits

Mind patterns can become entrenched unless they are challenged. Our flesh gets addicted to what it wants, but new habits can be formed. However, we will need to be intentional and aware of how and what we are thinking. We do not form good habits to try to achieve righteousness. Good habits are simply a part of our disciplined walk with God and will require us leading our flesh rather than following it. We can't use the excuse, "Well, I'm just not that type of person." The flesh is strong, but the more we practice the disciplines, the stronger God's Spirit becomes in us. Jesus showed us how to cultivate good habits. We can see how Jesus lived out good habits as well as what the Bible says about their formation.

Habit of Praying

"But Jesus often withdrew to lonely places and prayed" (Luke 5:16, NIV).

Habit of Consistency

"Each day Jesus was teaching at the temple, and each evening he went out to spend the night on the hill called the Mount of Olives," (Luke 21:37, NIV).

Habit of Trusting God in Suffering

Jesus continuously entrusted Himself and His welfare to God. "And while being abusively insulted, He did not insult in return; while suffering, He did not threaten, but kept entrusting Himself to Him who judges righteously;" (1 Peter 2:23, NASB).

Our Habits

Scripture exhorts us to make habits, too, regarding our mindset and behavior. These are done in Christ's strength and the power of the Holy Spirit. However, our free will also needs to make up our mind to pursue the mind of Christ.

Habit of Discernment

"But solid food is for the mature, who by constant use have trained themselves to distinguish good from evil" (Hebrews 5:14, NIV).

Habit of Behavior

"So whatever you say or whatever you do, remember that you will be judged by the law that sets you free" (James 2:12, NLT).

Habit of Worship

"Not neglecting to meet together, as is the habit of some, but encouraging one another, and all the more as you see the Day drawing nearer" (Hebrew 10:25, ESV).

Habit of a Repentant Lifestyle

"Therefore confess your sins to each other and pray for each other so that you may be healed. The prayer of a righteous person is powerful and effective" (James 5:16, NIV).

"If we confess our sins, he is faithful and just and will forgive us our sins and purify us from all unrighteousness" (1 John 1:9, NIV).

Our habits help to reinforce or tear down the mind of Christ. Habits are central to walking and living in the Spirit.

Trigger 3: Culture

We have been inundated with worldly mindsets since the day we were born. Countering these is hard but not impossible. We can adopt a new counterculture that is led by the Holy Spirit. When this is too hard for us, the Holy Spirit intercedes on our behalf: "And he who searches our hearts knows the mind of the Spirit, because the Spirit intercedes for God's people in accordance with the will of God" (Romans 8:27, NIV).

Trigger 4: Thinking in Our Own Strength

The mind of Christ is not an attempt at good works. We cannot manufacture such a mind. Trying to be a good person will never measure up. Putting confidence in our ability to figure things out will lead us into trouble, too. We must learn to depend on God's thoughts. They are trustworthy, and His Word is perfect.

Trigger 5: Sin

Plain and simple, sin hampers our ability to have the mind of Christ. Christ was sinless, and now in Christ we have a choice not to sin, enabled by the grace of God and the power of the Holy Spirit. "My little children, I am writing these things to you so that you may not sin. But if anyone does sin, we have an advocate with the Father, Jesus Christ the righteous" (1 John 2:1, ESV). Paul said we are not to continue in sin (Romans 6:1). However, so often we make excuses for our negative mindsets rather than tackling and overcoming them through putting on the mind of Christ. Friends, can we picture Jesus having any of the negative mindsets we give ourselves over to? Short answer: No. It makes us laugh at the thought, right? We may think, "Well, Jesus was perfect; He was God," to excuse us from living out the mind of Christ. But we have the mind of Christ, so why wouldn't we live into that reality?

Seeing Through Jesus' Eyes

Through Jesus' eyes and mind, we see things in the scope of eternity and God's purposes, not our own. The mind of Christ can feel so intangible and impossible when we strive and live according to our own understanding. But there is within us the ability to rise above. We have seen this mind of Christ in the pages of this book. We can now live it out.

Tip 1: Guard Our Mind

We must protect our mindset, friends. It is that space where our belief system is formed. We need to protect it from worldly influences and deception. The mind is under major attack. The secularization of our minds happens easily enough because we let it happen. We numb our minds with entertainment by scrolling through our phones endlessly or watching movies to escape our reality. But reality does not need to be escaped. It needs to be faced with Jesus. We have not been left alone to face this harsh world. We have the mind of Christ.

Tip 2: Self-Awareness

"Denise, practice self-awareness," my friend told me.

"Huh?" I asked. "What does that mean?"

"Actually," he said, "you do fine in that area."

But his statement made me think. He likely meant that I should be aware of how I was coming across to others. And while that has some importance, there is another self-awareness that is more critical. We live in our own bodies but are often not aware of the schemes our mindset is making. We need to recognize what direction our thought patterns are headed then direct them back to redeemed thoughts. Being in God's Word helps us make up our mind rather than having our mind made up for us.

Tip 3: Accountability

The Holy Spirit knows all things because He is God. This is the utmost in accountability, yet we can dodge the Holy Spirit and listen to the noise of the world. It is hard to hide from One who lives within us, right? In addition, we can let someone into our inner circle to help us with our negative mindsets. We need to give this person permission to speak into our lives though; otherwise, we might bite the bait of an offense and stay stuck in a mindset instead of living in the mind of Christ.

Tip 4: Saturation in God's Word

For the past seven years I have served as an executive and marketing assistant. My job has included helping my employer write most of his marketing communications. To be able to write for him, I had to learn my employer's thoughts. This took time and dedication as I studied his writing and message. So it is with Christ. We can't think like Christ if we don't know Him. The label of "Christian" is not like a membership to a club. It is family. We represent God Almighty on this earth.

I've told my kids they represent our family when they go out into the world. They also represent the family of God. Every person in a family is unique, but there are also characteristics that identify us as belonging together. In the family of God, if we are not spending time with Jesus, we won't look and act like Him. Spending intentional time studying and reading God's Word changes us supernaturally and transforms our thought patterns.

How many minutes of our day are spent being "mindless," getting distracted, scrolling through newsfeeds? Now how much time are we actually in the Word of God? We can get creative with influencing ourselves with the Word of God. Listening to worship music or Scripture on the way to work is a great way to saturate our minds. Meeting with others who are like-minded in Christ reinforces the principles of God in our mind and life as well.

Tip 5: Out with the Old, In with the New

It is hard to add new ways of thinking if we haven't debunked the old. Old wineskins can burst when new wine is added to them. Lies and truth cannot coexist. When we recognize the lies of the old mindsets and release them in Jesus' name, we make space for the new mind of Christ.

Getting to the Root

Our thoughts matter. They shape our life. We need to pay attention to negative mindsets and take captive thoughts that displease God. We need to protect our belief system. We who are in Christ have been given the mind of Christ. If we don't live it out, how will the world know Jesus?

Mindset of Christ

"But as He came closer to Jerusalem and saw the city ahead, he began to weep. 'How I wish today that you of all people would understand the way to peace. But now it is too late, and peace is hidden from your eyes'" (Luke 19:41-42, NLT).

Negative mindsets rob us of our peace. We misunderstand God's purposes and plans and can miss His way when we stay stuck in mindsets instead of reaching for the grace of God and the higher understanding available in the mind of Christ. Christ wept for people's lack of understanding. He has given us all we need. "His divine power has given us everything we need for a godly life through our knowledge of him who called us by his own glory and goodness" (2 Peter 1:3, NIV). When we struggle in our thoughts, all it takes is for us to cry out and ask Jesus for wisdom. He will give it. We don't have to stay stuck in our thoughts anymore. We have the mind of Christ.

Mind Renewal: Keys to Unlock Our Mind

Key Thought:

When we expose wrong thoughts, we are set free to have the peace that the mind of Christ brings.

Key Verse: Truth from God's Word

"The LORD's light penetrates the human spirit, exposing every hidden motive" (Proverbs 20:27, NLT).

Key Change: Application—Releasing Our Mindsets and Adopting Christ's

Looking over this exploration of negative mindsets and having the mind of Christ, we can ask God about what we need to let go of, journal our prayer requests, and pray for the Holy Spirit to reveal what inhibits us from walking in the mind of Christ. We can build the good habit of examining our thoughts because walking in the mind of Christ is not a once and done proposition. We need to renew our minds daily with the help of the Holy Spirit and God's precious Word. I would love to hear about your victories and your challenges as you learn to walk in the mind of Christ. Watch your thoughts, friends. They become mindsets and they shape your life and eternity. Go with God—He is always with you, for you, and in you.

Counselor's Corner

If you have chosen to believe and trust in Jesus and identify yourself as a Christian, you already have the mind of Christ (1 Corinthians 2:16). It's a gift that is already yours. When a client struggles with believing something is true about them, I use a counseling intervention I call "act as if." I'm not suggesting if you act as if you have a million dollars, your bank balance will suddenly display seven figures. But acting as if you have certain traits helps to empower you to live out the process of change by becoming more like the you whom you aspire to be.

For example, if you want to behave as if you are a calm person, you would first determine what you will think and how you will behave. For Christians, we are fortunate to have the added power of the Holy Spirit manifesting Himself in us. I ask God to allow me to envision who I am becoming in Christ. Then, I break down what that looks like for me practically.

- How does that woman wake up?
- What does she think about when she gets ready?
- How does she spend her money?
- How does she interact with people?
- What does she do with her free time?

These are a few examples of questions I ask myself when going through this process. Now let's apply this practice to the mind of Christ.

- What would the mind of Christ in you think when you first wake up?

- What would your morning routine look like with the mind of Christ?
- What would Christ say to you when you look in the mirror?
- What would His thoughts be as your kids are getting ready for school?
- What would the mind of Christ think when eating?
- How would the mind of Christ behave at work?

Can you get a glimpse of what you and your day would look like living out the mind of Christ? Devote some time to this exercise. See yourself living in the mind of Christ when interacting with people. The result will look different for each of us because of our uniqueness.

If I were to pick one theme of the women I interact with, it would be that we are so hard on ourselves. We tell ourselves truth without grace, and we rarely let the love of God cover our sins. These critical thoughts rob us of the life God created us to live. They rob us of a greater impact for the kingdom, and they prevent all the positive emotions we so desperately desire. But the Bible paints a repetitive picture of Christ approaching women with compassion—the woman at the well, the woman caught in adultery, and Martha, who got caught up in sweating the small stuff. The mind of Christ does not weigh us down; it frees us.

We have come to the end of our time together. I hope this book is only the beginning of our interactions. I'd love for you to share with me any interventions you try and how they have impacted your life. My desire in writing books like this one is to take the strategies our counselors have has been using behind closed doors for years and get them out into the church and community. In closing, I want to leave you with the same words I tell my clients at the end of their series of sessions with me, "I can't wait to hear about the difference this change in mindset will make in your life today and in the years to come." If you don't feel comfortable contacting me, I encourage you to share the changes you see God making in your life with someone. Testifying to His work in our lives reinforces transformation.

Mindset Movement 1: *Use the questions above as a mind of Christ exercise. Write your answers with as much detail as you possibly can. Review and edit it often, and share with someone you trust how it is changing the way you live.*

Mindset Movement 2: *Share with someone today your testimony of the transformation God has started in your life.*

Here again is the link to the "What's Your Mindset Struggle?" quiz: bit.ly/mindset-battle-quiz.

Endnotes

[1] Jerry Falwell Sr.

[2] "'Mind' in the Bible." Mind in the Bible (762 instances). Knowing-Jesus.com. https://bible.knowing-jesus.com/words/Mind.

[3] "'Thoughts' in the Bible." Thoughts in the Bible (195 instances). Knowing-Jesus.com. https://bible.knowing-jesus.com/words/Thoughts.

[4] Oxford University Press (2021) mindset. In: Lexico.com, Available at: https://www.lexico.com/definition/mindset [Accessed 02/11/22].

[5] Dreher, Beth, and Claire Nowak. "9 Split-Second Decisions That Changed History." Reader's Digest. Reader's Digest, August 4, 2021.

[6] Tackett, Del. "What's a Christian Worldview?" Focus on the Family, January 1, 2006. https://www.focusonthefamily.com/faith/whats-a-christian-worldview/.

[7] Oxford University Press (2021) mad. In: Lexico.com, Available at: https://www.lexico.com/definition/mad [Accessed 02/11/22].

[8] Taken from *Wishful thinking: A theological ABC* by Frederick Buechner (Nashville: Thomas Nelson, 1993) by Frederick Buchner. Used by permission of Thomas Nelson.

[9] Taken from *Forgiving What You Can't Forget* by Lysa TerKeurst (Nashville: Thomas Nelson, 2020) by Lysa TerKeurst. Used by permission of Thomas Nelson.

[10] Boritt, Gabor S. *Of the People, by the People, for the People: and Other Quotations from Abraham Lincoln*, (Columbia University Press, 1997), xvii.

[11] Ten Boom, Corrie. *The Hiding Place*, © 2006 Baker Publishing Group.

[12] Oswalt, John N. "940 בָּאַר." In *Theological Wordbook of the Old Testament*, ed. R. Laird Harris, Gleason L. Archer Jr., and Bruce K. Waltke, 425. Chicago: Moody Press, 1999.

[13] "Reproduced from "Depression." World Health Organization. World Health Organization, September 13, 2021. https://www.who.int/newsroom/fact-sheets/detail/depression.

[14] Craft, Lynette L., and Frank M. Perna. "The Benefits of Exercise for the Clinically Depressed." Primary care companion to the Journal of clinical psychiatry. Physicians Postgraduate Press, Inc., 2004. https://www.ncbi.nlm.nih.gov/pmc/articles/PMC474733/.

[15] "G4100 – pisteuō – Strong's Greek Lexicon (NASB)." Blue Letter Bible. Accessed 12 Feb, 2021. https://www.blueletterbible.org//lang/Lexicon/Lexicon.cfm?Strongs=G4100&t=NASB

[16] "G4100 – pisteuō – Strong's Greek Lexicon (NASB)." Blue Letter Bible. Accessed 12 Feb, 2021. https://www.blueletterbible.org//lang/Lexicon/Lexicon.cfm?Strongs=G4100&t=NASB

[17] "H3820 – lēḇ - Strong's Hebrew Lexicon (NASB)." Blue Letter Bible. Accessed 12 Feb, 2021. https://www.blueletterbible.org//lang/Lexicon/Lexicon.cfm?Strongs=H3820&t=NASB

[18] "'Believe' in the Bible." Believe in the Bible (267 instances). Knowing-Jesus.com. https://bible.knowing-jesus.com/words/Believe.
[19] Montgomery, Lucy Maud. *Anne of Green Gables.* L.C. Page & Co., 1908.
[20] Conzelmann, Hans and Walther Zimmerli, "Χαίρω, Χαρά, Συγχαίρω, Χάρις, Χαρίζομαι, Χαριτόω, Ἀχάριστος, Χάρισμα, Εὐχαριστέω, Εὐχαριστία, Εὐχάριστος," In *Theological Dictionary of the New Testament,* edited by Gerhard Kittel, Geoffrey W. Bromiley, and Gerhard Friedrich. Grand Rapids, 360. Grand Rapids, MI: Eerdmans, 1964.
[21] Ibid., 363.
[22] "H213 – 'ûṣ - Strong's Hebrew Lexicon (NASB)." Blue Letter Bible. Accessed 14 Feb, 2021. https://www.blueletterbible.org//lang/Lexicon/Lexicon.cfm?Strongs=H213&t=NASB
[23] Wolf, Herbert. "51 אוּץ." In *Theological Wordbook of the Old Testament,* edited by R. Laird Harris, Gleason L. Archer Jr., and Bruce K. Waltke. Chicago: Moody Press, 1999.
[24] H1847 – daʿaṯ - Strong's Hebrew Lexicon (NASB95)." Blue Letter Bible. Accessed 9 Mar, 2021. https://www.blueletterbible.org//lang/Lexicon/Lexicon.cfm?Strongs=H1847&t=NASB95
[25] MindTools.com. *How to Beat Hurry Sickness: Overcoming Constant Panic and Rush* [Online]. Available from: https://www.mindtools.com/pages/article/how-to-beat-hurry-sickness.htm. [Accessed: 1/11/22].
[26] Taken from *The Life You've Always Wanted: Spiritual Disciplines for Ordinary People* by John Ortberg. Copyright © 1997 by John Ortberg, p. 84. Used by permission of Thomas Nelson.
[27] "G4049 – perispaō – Strong's Greek Lexicon (NASB)." Blue Letter Bible. Accessed 15 Feb, 2021. https://www.blueletterbible.org//lang/Lexicon/Lexicon.cfm?Strongs=G4049&t=NASB
[28] Vine, W. "Cumber – Vines Expository Dictionary of New Testament Words." Blue Letter Bible. Last Modified 24 Jun, 1996. https://www.blueletterbible.org/search/dictionary/viewtopic.cfm
[29] Taken from *Romans: The NIV Application Commentary: From Biblical Text to Contemporary Life* by Douglas Moo Copyright © 2000 by Douglas Moo, p. 215. Used by permission of Zondervan.
[30] Taken from *The Best Yes: Making Wise Decisions in the Midst of Endless Demands* by Lysa TerKeurst. Copyright © 2014 by Lysa TerKeurst, p. 18. Used by permission of Thomas Nelson.
[31] "H3173 – yāḥîḏ - Strong's Hebrew Lexicon (NASB)." Blue Letter Bible. Accessed 15 Feb, 2021. https://www.blueletterbible.org//lang/Lexicon/Lexicon.cfm?Strongs=H3173&t=NASB
[32] "G5207 – yhios – Strong's Greek Lexicon (KJV)." Blue Letter Bible. Accessed 15 Feb, 2021. https://www.blueletterbible.org//lang/lexicon/lexicon.cfm?Strongs=G5207&t=KJV
[33] Gilchrist, Paul R. "858 דַּחַי." In *Theological Wordbook of the Old Testament,* edited by R. Laird Harris, Gleason L. Archer Jr., and Bruce K. Waltke. Chicago: Moody Press, 1999.

[34] Whitwer, Glynnis. "Turning Thanksgiving into Thanksgiving." November 18, 2013. http://glynniswhitwer.com/2013/11/turning-thanksgiving-into-thanks-sharing/
[35] "Psalm 10 (NASB) - Why do You stand afar." Blue Letter Bible. Accessed 26 Feb, 2021. https://www.blueletterbible.org/nasb/psa/10/1/ss1/s_488001
[36] Culver, Robert D. "2095 האָר." In *Theological Wordbook of the Old Testament*, edited by Harris, R. Laird, Gleason L. Archer Jr., and Bruce K. Waltke, 823. Chicago: Moody Press, 1999.
[37] "'Repent' in the Bible." Repent in the Bible (93 instances). Knowing-Jesus.com. Accessed February 11, 2022. https://bible.knowing-jesus.com/words/Repent.
[38] "'Repentance' in the Bible." Repentance in the Bible (40 instances). Knowing-Jesus.com. Accessed February 11, 2022. https://bible.knowing-jesus.com/words/Repentance.
[39] "G3340 - metanoeō - Strong's Greek Lexicon (NASB95)." Blue Letter Bible. Accessed 11 Mar, 2021. https://www.blueletterbible.org//lang/Lexicon/Lexicon.cfm?Strongs=G3340&t=NASB95
[40] "G4100 - pisteuō - Strong's Greek Lexicon (NASB95)." Blue Letter Bible. Accessed 11 Mar, 2021. https://www.blueletterbible.org//lang/Lexicon/Lexicon.cfm?Strongs=G4100&t=NASB95
[41] Georg Bertram, "Στρέφω, Ἀναστρέφω, Ἀναστροφή, Καταστρέφω, Καταστροφή, Διαστρέφω, Ἀποστρέφω, Ἐπιστρέφω, Ἐπιστροφή, Μεταστρέφω," In *Theological Dictionary of the New Testament*, edited by Gerhard Kittel, Geoffrey W. Bromiley, and Gerhard Friedrich. Grand Rapids, 727. Grand Rapids, MI: Eerdmans, 1964.
[42] Johannes Behm and Ernst Würthwein, "Νοέω, Νοῦς, Νόημα, Ἀνόητος, Ἄνοια, Δυσνόητος, Διάνοια, Διανόημα, Ἔννοια, Εὐνοέω, Εὔνοια, Κατανοέω, Μετανοέω, Μετάνοια, Ἀμετανόητος, Προνοέω, Πρόνοια, Ὑπονοέω, Ὑπόνοια, Νουθετέω, Νουθεσία," In *Theological Dictionary of the New Testament*, edited by Gerhard Kittel, Geoffrey W. Bromiley, and Gerhard Friedrich. Grand Rapids, 966. Grand Rapids, MI: Eerdmans, 1964.
[43] Taken from *Romans: The NIV Application Commentary: From Biblical Text to Contemporary Life* by Douglas Moo Copyright © 2000 by Douglas Moo, p. 215–216. Used by permission of Zondervan.
[44] "H7307 - rûaḥ - Strong's Hebrew Lexicon (KJV)." Blue Letter Bible. Accessed 27 Feb, 2021. https://www.blueletterbible.org//lang/Lexicon/Lexicon.cfm?Strongs=H7307&t=KJV
[45] Johannes Behm and Ernst Würthwein, "Νοέω, Νοῦς, Νόημα, Ἀνόητος, Ἄνοια, Δυσνόητος, Διάνοια, Διανόημα, Ἔννοια, Εὐνοέω, Εὔνοια, Κατανοέω, Μετανοέω, Μετάνοια, Ἀμετανόητος, Προνοέω, Πρόνοια, Ὑπονοέω, Ὑπόνοια, Νουθετέω, Νουθεσία." In *Theological Dictionary of the New Testament*, edited by Gerhard Kittel, Geoffrey W. Bromiley, and Gerhard Friedrich. Grand Rapids, 967. Grand Rapids, MI: Eerdmans, 1964.